# LET'S STUDY
# GALATIANS

*Series Editor:* SINCLAIR B. FERGUSON

# Let's Study
# GALATIANS

Derek Thomas

THE BANNER OF TRUTH TRUST

THE BANNER OF TRUTH TRUST
3 Murrayfield Road, Edinburgh EH12 6EL, UK
P.O. Box 621, Carlisle, PA 17013, USA

\*

© Derek Thomas 2004
First Published 2004
Reprinted 2009

ISBN-13: 978 0 85151 876 3

\*

Scripture quotations are from THE HOLY BIBLE,
ENGLISH STANDARD VERSION, © Copyright 2001 by
Crossway Bibles, a division of Good News Publishers.
Used by permission.
All rights reserved.

Typeset in 11/12.5 pt Ehrhardt MT at the
Banner of Truth Trust, Edinburgh

Printed in the U.S.A. by
Versa Press, Inc.,
East Peoria, IL

TO

DAVID AND ANDREA
JUSSELY

# Contents

# Publisher's Preface

*L*et's *Study Galatians* is part of a series of books which explain and apply the message of Scripture. The series is designed to meet a specific and important need in the church. While not technical commentaries, the volumes comment on the text of a biblical book; and, without being merely lists of practical applications, they are concerned with the ways in which the teaching of Scripture can affect and transform our lives today. Understanding the Bible's message and applying its teaching are the aims.

Like other volumes in the series, *Let's Study Galatians* seeks to combine explanation and application. Its concern is to be helpful to ordinary Christian people by encouraging them to understand the message of the Bible and apply it to their own lives. The reader in view is not the person who is interested in all the detailed questions which fascinate the scholar, although behind the writing of each study lies an appreciation for careful and detailed scholarship. The aim is exposition of Scripture written in the language of a friend, seated alongside you with an open Bible.

*Let's Study Galatians* is designed to be used in various contexts. It can be used simply as an aid for individual Bible study. Some may find it helpful to use in their devotions with husband or wife, or to read in the context of the whole family.

In order to make these studies more useful, not only for individual use but also for group study in Sunday School classes and home, church or college, study guide material will be found on pp. 167–84. Sometimes we come away frustrated rather than helped by group discussions. Frequently that is because we have been encouraged to discuss a passage of Scripture which we do not understand very well in the first place. Understanding must always be the foundation for enriching discussion and for thoughtful, practical application. Thus, in addition to the exposition of Galatians, the additional material provides questions to encourage personal thought and study, or to be used as discussion starters. The Group Study Guide divides the material into thirteen sections and provides direction for leading and participating in group study and discussion.

# *Acknowledgements*

Having submitted a previous volume in this series, *Let's Study Revelation*, I was asked if I might consider submitting another on Galatians. Paul's first epistle is only six chapters, as opposed to John's Apocalypse which has twenty-two. The decision was relatively easy! But I have to admit to finding Galatians a great challenge, as has anyone who has wrestled with the heart of Paul's understanding of justification by faith alone.

In recent years there has emerged an entirely 'new' understanding of Paul's teaching, of Galatians, and of justification in particular. It is hardly possible these days to read literature on Paul without confronting the strident claims of this 'new perspective'.

I would like to acknowledge the help of Dr Guy Waters for invaluable insights into this issue. His lectures on 'The New Perspective on Paul' have been invaluable to me.

Several of these chapters at one time found an existence in another form–as 'Bible Studies' to several adult Bible classes at First Presbyterian Church, Jackson, where I serve as Minister of Teaching. Working with its senior minister, Dr Ligon Duncan, and more importantly, learning from him, is an immeasurable treasure.

Various people have helped me in the production of this volume including a gracious secretary, Ruth Bennett, at (what is my 'day' job!) Reformed Theological Seminary, Jackson. My longsuffering Thornwell assistant, John Tweeddale, offered invaluable help even though marriage to his bride-to-be Angela loomed ever closer on the horizon.

It is never possible to accomplish these 'extra' things without the long-suffering encouragement of my wife and partner for twenty-eight years. Rosemary is a gift from God which I do not deserve.

Friends are precious. For the past thirty years, I have known and respected David Jussely. In recent years we have been colleagues-professors at Reformed Theological Seminary. He is also my neighbour. Most evenings, we walk (or are walked by) our respective canine companions, Jake and Smokey. On these sultry evenings in Mississippi, we have conversed on almost every topic imaginable and have always found agreement – well, apart that is from a fondness for grits! David and his dear wife Andrea are models of 'Southern comfort'! It is to them that I dedicate this volume.

DEREK THOMAS

# Introduction

A certain tradition states that Galatians was Paul's first letter. It bears all the signs of a young convert's zeal. Its tone is blunt and sometimes indignant. It can seem alarmingly straightforward, but it also reveals deeper layers of immense significance.

There is no other letter of Paul's quite like this one. There is none of the warmth and charm that exudes from the pages of Philippians, for example. One theme seems to envelop him and he seems hardly able to address anything else. The very gospel is at stake.

In what seems like a relatively short period of time since their conversion (*Gal.* 1:6), the Galatian believers have turned away from the teaching of the apostle to embrace something which he regards as damnable. The stakes could hardly be higher.

Nor is Paul in a position to exert his authority without a great deal of defence on his part. Indeed, it takes him almost a chapter and a half to get to the issue that evidently burns within him – *justification*! And then, having got to it, he seems unable to let it go! Little wonder that Luther, at the dawn of the Reformation in Europe, found in Galatians something that resonated in his own soul. He would write of this letter, 'The Epistle to the Galatians is my Epistle. I have betrothed myself to it; it is my wife.'

## AN EARLY CRISIS IN THE CHURCH

It is hardly possible to read any line of Galatians without appreciating that a major crisis has broken out in the relationship between the apostle Paul and the churches he founded in Galatia. What exactly has happened? When Paul first went to Galatia, the apostle felt as though they 'would have gouged out (their) eyes and given them to me' (4:15). But something has happened to create distrust. Who it is exactly who has stirred up this opposition is not clear. At one point, Paul seems to suggest that a single individual lies behind it (5:10).

The issue was the acceptance of Gentiles into the Church. Were they obligated to observe those 'markers' of Jewishness: circumcision, kosher food laws and the Sabbath? It must have been difficult for Jewish Christians to come to terms with the radical nature of new covenant Christianity. Some who were deeply suspicious of the ease with which Gentiles were 'accepted', began insisting upon compliance with markers of synagogue fellowship. It was a recipe for tension.

Things are further complicated by the seemingly sinister tactic of pitting the Jerusalem church against the church at Antioch. Jerusalem was the mother church of the New Testament. It was there that the chief apostles (John, Peter and James) resided. As the letter unfolds, a tangled web of conspiracy emerges: what appears to have been an agreement between the men from Antioch (Paul and Barnabas) and the men in Jerusalem (John, Peter, James) had quickly broken down. A catastrophic visit by Peter to Antioch resulted in a hot and very public face-off with Paul. It must have been an occasion that remained in the memories and conversations of those who witnessed it for the rest of their lives!

## WHERE AND WHEN?

Two intriguing questions arise in connection with this letter. To whom was Galatians written? And when? Scholars divide into advocates of a 'Northern Galatian' or a 'Southern Galatian' view! Added to this intriguing debate is a second issue: was it written *before* or *after* the Jerusalem Council of Acts 15? The fact that the issues debated in the Jerusalem Council are similar to the ones that arise in this epistle makes it odd – if the letter was written *after* the Council – that Paul never mentions it, or its resolutions, at any point in the unfolding argument of the letter.

At the risk of over-simplification, the issues involved are these:

1. Paul addressed the letter to 'the churches in Galatia' (1:2).
Patristic, medieval and Reformation commentators argued that the
name Galatia properly referred to a region in the north of present-
day Turkey (in which the cities of Ancyra, Pessinus and Tavium
were found). These Galatians were the descendants of the Celtic
tribes which had conquered the region in the third century BC.

Those who hold this view take the references in Acts 16:6 ('the
region of Phrygia and Galatia') and 18:23 ('the region of Galatia
and Phrygia') as Paul's missionary expeditions to North Galatia.
This necessarily requires a date for the writing of the letter that is
after these missionary journeys, that is, *after* Acts 18:23. This
would make it, at the very earliest, around 53 AD.

2. Other scholars have adopted the view that Galatians was
written to those churches established as a result of Paul's first
missionary journey, recorded in Acts 13 and 14, the region of
Pisidian Antioch, Iconium, Lystra and Derbe. In this case, Acts
16:6 and 18:23 refer to Paul's return to South Galatia. Whilst the
people of these regions were not true Galatians (by race), they were
regarded as such by the Roman Empire. This implies that
Galatians could have been written much earlier, immediately after
the first missionary journey. Thus Galatians could have been have
been written as early as 49 AD.

3. Of even greater complexity is the identification of Paul's visit
to Jerusalem referred to in 2:1. 'Then after fourteen years I went
up again to Jerusalem with Barnabas, taking Titus along with me.'
In fact Acts refers to no less than five visits by Paul to Jerusalem.
Yet none of them seems to correspond to the details of the one
recorded in Galatians 2. Two principal contenders have arisen
which identify the visit in Galatians 2 with either Acts 11:27–30 or
15:1–30. Identifying the visit with the occasion of the Jerusalem
Council makes sense in that the same (or at least similar) concerns
were then at issue. But it is strange that neither Luke nor Paul
equate the two occasions precisely.

Defenders of the Acts 15 point of view have brought forward
convincing arguments, which include the view that Paul did not
appeal to the decree, even though it had been issued, because he

had no need to do so. His authority lay in his apostolic office, not in the decree of the Jerusalem Council. But it is then difficult to understand Peter's withdrawal from table fellowship at Antioch if the Jerusalem Council had already issued its verdict that Gentiles were under no obligation to comply with kosher food laws.

Others (including the present writer, on the whole!) maintain that Paul's Galatian 2 visit to Jerusalem is the one recorded in Acts 11, 'the famine-relief visit'. But this viewpoint also is subject to similar criticisms. Why did Paul not mention the issue of famine relief (compare Acts 11:30)? Why did Luke not mention the meeting of the Council referred to Galatians 2?

Important as all of this is if we are to do justice to the historical context of both Luke's and Paul's record of events, nothing essential is at issue. These studies will try to be sensitive to both the early and the later date, while its sympathies reside with the earlier one.

## A 'NEW PERSPECTIVE ON PAUL'

An important issue has arisen in the study of Paul's writings, one that has gained increasing significance in recent decades. A 'new perspective' has been proposed in the interpretation of Paul. It has called into question an interpretation that has been in vogue from Luther onwards (and that, according to some of us, goes back to Augustine in the fifth century).

The roots of this 'new' interpretation are found in the late nineteenth century, but it did not gain serious acceptance until the publication, in 1977, of a work entitled *Paul and Palestinian Judaism* by E. P. Sanders. Since then a movement has arisen, popularised by James D. G. Dunn and more recently N. T. Wright, that critiques in strident tones past interpretations of *justification by faith* and therefore also of *righteousness* and of *covenant*.

The movement has many twists and turns and does not speak with one voice. In one sense there is no such thing as '*the* new perspective on Paul.' But a trend can be discerned and it is impossible to ignore it.

What is this 'new perspective'? At its centre, it is a perspective critical of both Protestant and Catholic interpretations of Paul. It claims that Reformation-era theologians read medieval categories into first-century Judaism. Expressions like 'the righteousness of God,' 'the works of the law,' 'imputation,' and especially 'justification' were understood within a framework of late medieval merit theology. But, it is claimed, this was an alien concept to first-century Palestinian Jews. They did not employ a works-righteousness understanding of salvation (*How much do I need to do in order to be saved?*). Thus, it is argued, the idea of *earning* salvation by good works, while relevant in the sixteenth-century debates between Luther and Rome, is wholly out of place when thinking of Paul's debate with the Judaizers.

What then is the concern of the apostle with Judaism? The answer, it is suggested, is one of *inclusion*. Some Jewish believers were too narrow in their understanding of who belonged to the kingdom. Paul's mission was to convince them that Gentiles, as well as Jews, belong to the kingdom.

Such a view, as we have said, has far reaching implications. In making the point of discussion one of *ecclesiology* (who *belongs* to God's church) rather than *soteriology* (how a person *enters* the church), the focus shifts entirely. No longer is Paul talking about the saved and the lost, but about membership in the outward visible community. The issue then is not legalism but ethno-centrism. Paul is addressing a form of racism!

There can be no denying that something of this issue existed in the churches of Galatia. Jewish Christians were finding it difficult to think of un-circumcised Gentiles as fellow members of the same community. Indeed, the place of circumcision, certain food laws and table fellowship, as well as the observance of the Jewish Sabbath, were issues of great concern in this emerging New Testament Church.

But in defending a traditional (Reformational) understanding of justification, it will be necessary from time to time to highlight the issue of Gentile inclusion without in any way acceding to the tenets of this new interpretation. We will address this issue further in the course of our studies.

At the dawn of the third millennium, the pages of Galatians still resonate with freshness and power. The church is vastly more complicated and certainly more diverse than it was in these fledgling days of the New Testament. But with these words the voice of the Holy Spirit still speaks to issues of today – issues of conviction, of truth, of the very gospel itself. Those who find its contents too strident, too judgemental have themselves been 'bewitched' (3:1) by the post-modernity of this 'present evil age' (1:4). Nothing therefore could be more relevant than a study of this letter.

# *Outline of Galatians*

1. INTRODUCTION

   i.     Opening Greetings (1:1–5)
   ii.    Paul's Denunciation (1: 6–10)

2. DEFENCE OF PAUL'S APOSTLESHIP

   i.     Received by Revelation (1:11–12)
   ii.    Independent of Jerusalem Apostles (1:13–2:21)

3. DEFENCE OF JUSTIFICATION BY FAITH

   i.     The Experience of the Galatians (3:1–5)
   ii.    Abraham (3:6–14)
   iii.   The Permanence of the Promise (3:15–18)
   iv.   The Purpose of the Law (3:19–4:7)
   v.    Paul's Concern for the Galatians (4:8–20)
   vi.   Appeal from Allegory (4:21–31)

4. DEFENCE OF CHRISTIAN LIBERTY

   i.     Liberty and Law (5:1–12)
   ii.    Liberty and Licence (5:13–26)
   iii.   Liberty to Love (6:1–10)

      a. Responsibility toward the Weak and Sinful (6:1–5)
      b. Responsibility toward the Leaders (6:6–9)
      c. Responsibility toward All People (6:10)

## 5. CONCLUSION

# I

# The Present Evil Age

*Paul, an apostle – not from men nor through man, but through Jesus Christ and God the Father, who raised him from the dead – ² and all the brothers who are with me,*
*To the churches of Galatia: ³ Grace to you and peace from God our Father and the Lord Jesus Christ, ⁴ who gave himself for our sins to deliver us from the present evil age, according to the will of our God and Father, ⁵ to whom be the glory forever and ever. Amen (Gal. 1:1–5).*

There is something of the energy of a young convert about this letter. Galatians was probably Paul's first apostolic letter. More than likely it was written from his 'base of operations', Antioch, in 48 or 49 AD. In it, Paul defends the gospel of justification by grace against its detractors. Less than two decades have passed since the death and resurrection of Jesus and already, the fledgling church, now spreading north and west, is in significant trouble. Error of the most pernicious sort has infected the churches in Galatia.

A millennium and a half later, at the dawn of the sixteenth-century Reformation in central Europe, Martin Luther expressed his affinity with this letter. In his famous commentary on Galatians he wrote, 'If this doctrine be lost, then is also the doctrine of truth, life, and salvation, also lost and gone.' There is something in this letter, then, of fundamental importance.

## AUTHOR'S CREDENTIALS
Unlike our letters, which tend to end with the writer's name, ancient letters began with the author's name. In this letter, however,

something a little unusual follows. Paul immediately digresses in order to underline his authority.

It sounds as though Paul is throwing his weight around in this introduction, demanding attention because he is someone special – an *apostle*! But such a criticism is too simplistic. To tackle issues as important as the understanding of the gospel, Paul *needs* to defend his credentials. There were some who doubted his authority to speak on such important matters, since he was not 'one of the twelve'. But he *is* an 'apostle' nevertheless, and commands a hearing (1:1).

And what is so significant about an apostle? This: that it was an office instituted directly by God rather than men. Teachers often arrived in the cities of the ancient world with letters of recommendation from a notable dignitary or recognized authority. Paul claims divine approval for his role among the Galatians. He was sent '*not from men nor through man, but through Jesus Christ and God the Father*' (1:1). His authority is not derived from any human instrument, either in origin ('*from men*') or in mediation ('*through man*'). Paul is 'an apostle of Jesus Christ *by the will of God*' (*2 Cor.* 1:1).

This claim would come as a shock to some of his readers who had perhaps heard of an 'ordination' ritual that had taken place in Antioch when Saul and Barnabas had been 'set apart' for gospel ministry. But as Luke records so carefully, they had set him apart because the Holy Spirit had told them to (*Acts* 13:1–2). The truth is, Paul had been an apostle *before* this event in Antioch. In other words, these Galatian readers need to pay attention to what follows because Paul is not just another 'missionary'; he is an apostle – an emissary and spokesman on behalf of God!

Several features of this introduction are worth elaborating. The word 'apostle' means 'one who is sent'. The New Testament uses this word in both a general and specific sense. In the general sense, a man like Epaphroditus is called a 'messenger' (literally, 'apostle,' *Phil.* 2:25). Similarly, those commissioned by the Macedonian churches to aid Paul in distributing money to the poor in Jerusalem are also called 'messengers' (literally, 'apostles,' *2 Cor.* 8:23). Translations recognize that they are not 'apostles' in the strict sense and therefore use the word 'messenger' or 'representative' at these points.

In the sense that Paul uses 'apostle,' the term is reserved for those individuals who had both *seen*, and received a commission from, the risen Christ (see *Acts* 1:22). That explains in part why Paul places Jesus' name before that of the Father in the first verse, and why he goes on to say that Jesus was '*raised . . . from the dead*'. It is the resurrected Christ who set Paul apart as an apostle.

*When* did Paul see the risen Jesus? Writing to the Corinthians a few years later, Paul describes how Jesus 'appeared' to him (*1 Cor.* 15:8). The incident is recorded for us in Acts (*Acts* 9:1–8). The manner of this 'appearance' was unusual, and Paul describes himself as one who was 'untimely born', in the sense that he had not been a member of the original apostolic band. He had not lived with Jesus as the others had. Moreover, since Saul of Tarsus (as Paul was known before his conversion) had gained a reputation for being a violent man, his claim to apostleship was treated with scepticism by some and downright disdain by others.

## READERS: THE CHURCHES OF GALATIA

The Galatians are addressed as '*the churches of Galatia*' (1:2). Usually, in Paul's letters, there would follow some item of praise. But not here! He is in no mood for pleasantries. There is however the customary 'greeting': '*Grace to you and peace from God our Father and the Lord Jesus Christ*' (1:3).

Where exactly was Galatia? Three things are worth noting:

1.  Galatia was a *region* not a *place*. The province of Galatia has a rich and fascinating history. At some point in the distant past vast numbers of people from central Europe migrated to such regions as Britain (the Celts), the Balkans, and Asia Minor (that is, Galatia). Galatia grew in size as a province of Rome during and after New Testament times. Until recently, commentators assumed Galatia referred to the northern territories (the region that would eventually be called Galatia) even though not a single city in this region is mentioned either in the epistle itself or, more significantly, in Acts! There still are, however, advocates of the view that Galatia refers to this northern region.

Far more probable is the 'southern region view', which would make Galatia synonymous with the region containing Lystra, Iconium and Derbe – cities visited on Paul's missionary journey with Barnabas just over a year before the writing of this epistle.

2. More than one church is being addressed. '*Churches*' (1:2) implies that the infection concerning the understanding of the gospel, of which Paul will write, has affected more than one congregation. These assemblies have collectively succumbed to a deadly doctrinal infection.

Though the word *churches* can mean simply *assemblies*, and was regularly used this way for secular gatherings, it is also a word that has specific and important Old Testament roots. The Greek word *ecclesia* translates a Hebrew verb meaning '*to call*'. The church has been separated from the world into a grouping with a particular identity and calling. The word is in the plural here, *churches*. But it is also used elsewhere in the singular to suggest the *unity* of the church. It is essentially *one* entity ('the church throughout all Judea and Galilee and Samaria', *Acts* 9:31; see *Eph.* 4:3–6). Paul does just this in verse 13 when he recalls how he had persecuted 'the church of God.' Thus while there are individual churches in particular locations, it is also possible to speak of 'the church' collectively, the one church militant on earth.

Whatever implication we may wish to draw about the individuality of these churches, they are being addressed with one voice and expected to respond in identical terms. Their individuality does not mean total independence from each other. They are not at liberty to tamper with those truths that identify them as 'the church of God'.

3. We probably need to adjust our idea of what these 'churches' looked like. They would have had no buildings that might help identify them. The number of people in each church was probably fairly small. They might have appeared fairly disorganized by later standards: the offices of elder and deacon, and, more particularly, of someone who might be thought of as a 'minister' (teaching elder) were still embryonic. And more importantly, these early Christians would find themselves in tension and often in conflict with their culture and setting. Identifying themselves as 'Christians' (see *Acts* 11:26) would have been costly.

## GREETINGS

The rest of this opening section of the letter follows the conventional letter format. All is not well however and tension abounds in the very opening sentence! Two things that Paul does *not* say shout for our attention:

1. He says that the letter comes from him and certain 'brothers' (1:2). Who are these 'brothers'? The short answer is, *we don't know*! But it is very interesting (and perhaps *telling*) that Barnabas is not one of them – at least, Paul does not mention him by name. When he writes to the Thessalonians, he includes Silas and Timothy; when he writes his 'first' canonical letter to the Corinthians he includes Sosthenes; and on the 'second' occasion he includes Timothy. Since Barnabas had been with Paul whenever the gospel had first been preached in Galatia (*Acts* 13:43, 46, 50; 14:12, 14, 20), it would have made sense for Paul to mention him now. But a rift had developed between Paul and Barnabas (and Peter!) over meal practices whenever Gentiles were present. We shall have to examine this more carefully later (see *Gal.* 2:11–21, especially the reference to Barnabas at verse 13).

Barnabas was greatly loved and admired and it would have helped Paul enormously to have mentioned him here, particularly since he is desirous of their allegiance to what he was about to say. But Barnabas, too, has done something to compromise the gospel, and Paul can only make mention of 'brothers'. Anonymous as this reference is, at least it is in the plural! Paul is not alone.

2. As the early Church Father, Chrysostom, noted: Paul does not address the Galatians with any word of endearment. He called the Ephesians and Colossians 'faithful' (*Eph.* 1:1; *Col.* 1:1), and the Corinthians, 'sanctified' (*1 Cor.* 1:1). But there is nothing of that sort here. There is tension in the air!

These things notwithstanding, Paul wishes them grace and peace. *Grace* is God's love for the unworthy. To be precise, as Paul goes on to make clear, it is God's love for those who deserve condemnation. It is revealed to us most clearly in Christ, who '*gave himself for our sins*' (1:4). *Peace* echoes what would have been a familiar Hebrew greeting to many, *shalom*, physical and spiritual well-being. For Paul it relates to what is experienced when the fundamental relationship of alienation between man and God has been rectified through the cross and regeneration.

Our salvation is dependent upon the sovereignty of God *alone*. It is according to the '*will of our God and Father*' (1:4), and all the 'glory' is his, '*to whom be glory for ever and ever. Amen*' (1:5).

*Glory* is another Old Testament word. Its root meaning is to be heavy – it conveys the idea of weight, worth, significance, splendour and dignity. God wants us to extol him for what he is, for what he has done, and for what he will do. In our salvation we praise *him*, not ourselves or anyone else.

Several things are worth noting:

i. The work of Christ *for* us and *in* us is intimately connected with '*sin*'. That 'want of conformity unto, or transgression of the law of God' (*The Shorter Catechism*) is the root of all our trouble. It is not personality, or *karma*, or deprivation, that is the ultimate problem; it is sin. It is that lack of conformity to God's law in act, habit, attitude, outlook, disposition, and motivation that lies at the heart of our need for a Saviour and Deliverer. Christ deals with the problem of both sin (in the singular: a bad heart) and sins (as here in the plural: a bad record).

ii. Christ delivers us from '*the present evil age*'. The gospel has in view not only our personal regeneration and conversion, but also our ultimate glorification. It prepares us and equips us for 'the age to come' (*Matt.* 12:32; *Mark* 10:30; *Luke* 18:30; *Heb.* 6:5). We are pilgrims already tasting a part of the new creation (*2 Cor.* 5:20–21). The indwelling of the Holy Spirit as the 'seal' (*2 Cor.* 1:22) assures us of our share in the glory to come (*Rom.* 8:17). We are marching toward that eternal city 'whose designer and builder is God' (*Heb.* 11:10).

iii. Paul's use of 'Lord' in the expression 'the Lord Jesus Christ' (1:3) does not impact us in quite the same way as it would first-century readers. Paul is using the word *kurios* which could mean merely a polite 'Sir'. But for Paul it meant decidedly more. It was the word employed in the Greek translation of the Old Testament (the Septuagint) for the divine name of God – *Yahweh*! Every devout Jew affirmed daily that God is one by reciting the *Shema* of Deuteronomy 6:4, 'Hear, O Israel: The Lord our God, the Lord is one.' And Paul is adding that there is more than one who is the one God!

It is sometimes possible to discern that something is wrong from the first words of a letter. Paul has expressed no dissent. He has voiced no criticism. But something is wrong. You can sense it. To borrow the feeling of Shakespeare's *Hamlet*, there is 'something rotten' in the state of Galatia.

But what exactly?

**2**

# When Not to Believe an Angel

*I am astonished that you are so quickly deserting him who called*
*you in the grace of Christ and are turning to a different gospel –*
*⁷ not that there is another one, but there are some who trouble*
*you and want to distort the gospel of Christ. ⁸ But even if we or*
*an angel from heaven should preach to you a gospel contrary to*
*the one we preached to you, let him be accursed. ⁹ As we have*
*said before, so now I say again: If anyone is preaching to you a*
*gospel contrary to the one you received, let him be accursed*
(Gal. 1:6–9).

Curses! Paul has barely said 'hello' and 'trust you are well', and already he is calling down curses!

It is hard to imagine what these Galatians must have thought when they first heard this letter read. No doubt it passed around the various congregations, separated by many miles – taking several days, or even weeks, before it reached the final one. Perhaps word spread even before the letter arrived that Paul had written something very strong indeed. His opponents were no doubt confirmed in their suspicions of him. And Paul's admirers were nervous. What in the world has happened to bring Paul to call down a curse upon the Galatians? And what right does he have to do this? What is the problem?

## A DIFFERENT GOSPEL

To be fair, Paul is not speaking about all the Galatians, just a few of them – preachers who were preaching a *different* gospel, to be precise. But even so, he is accusing the Galatians collectively of *desertion* from the pure gospel which he had preached among them. What exactly were they now hearing, and how long had it been since Paul was there himself? We can take the second question first.

1. Dating Galatians is difficult for a variety of reasons but there is an incident – a visit to Jerusalem – alluded to in chapter 2 that may help us. Assuming that this incident (a second visit to Jerusalem fourteen years after the first visit, see 2:1) is the one mentioned in Acts 11:27–30 (the visit made by Paul and Barnabas for poverty relief), this would have been in the year 48 or 49 AD (the first missionary journey took place in 48 AD). Galatians was then written *some* time after that. Paul seems surprised that they succumbed to erroneous views '*so quickly*' (1:6). That could mean that Galatians was written towards the end of 49 or early in 50 AD.

Others equate this 'visit' with the Jerusalem Council recorded in Acts 15: 1–29. This would require a later date for Galatians and is a view often held together with the belief that the churches of Galatia were in the north, so that the letter was written after the third missionary journey (see *Acts* 18:23). According to this view, Galatians may have been written almost a decade later (around 57–58 AD). Some have conjectured that Paul wrote it from Ephesus around 55 AD (see *Acts* 19).

Whatever the *exact* date, Paul regards it as unnervingly soon after his visit there. Error takes hold with alarming speed. No sooner had Paul left them than some had begun to question the truth of what he had said. Constant vigilance is needed in maintaining the truth of the gospel.

2. But *what* exactly was being taught that had the apostle so hot under the collar? Why does he regard some of the Galatian believers as *deserters*? And lest things be thought personal (how could they not be?), Paul makes it clear that the one being deserted is God, not Paul! They are deserting the one who called them. They '*have fallen away from grace*' (5:4). Paul is not intending to suggest that true believers had, to quote the phrase, 'fallen from grace', in the sense that they were losing their salvation. His concern is theological: some who once had adopted his presentation of the gospel were now accepting another – an entirely different one in which 'grace' was missing. Whether they had been true believers or not is not the issue here.

Paul wants to make it clear that accepting this '*different*' view will bring the curse of God upon them. If they adopt this different gospel, then, as far as Paul is concerned, they have forfeited any claim to being considered true members of the church of God. It is as serious as that.

## GRACE

The clue to what is at stake comes in the phrase '*the grace of Christ*' (1:6). The gospel is all about *grace* and *Jesus Christ*. For Paul, the gospel is a God-centred way of thinking about man's condition and God's remedy. Sin is so radical in its nature that only undeserved mercy can deal with it. At the heart of the cheapening of grace by the Galatians lies an inadequate appreciation of the human condition. Their failure to see deep into the problem led to their myopic view of the solution. The gravitational pull of self-justification, in whatever precise form it comes, is very strong; indeed, it is an instinct that only a sovereign work of God can remedy. Grace is not only mercy; it is also a *power* that *brings salvation* (see *Titus* 2:11). We will have to examine the issue in greater detail as this epistle unfolds, but already we are given a foretaste of things to come: the Galatians have lost sight of their need for grace.

## ONE WAY

Any presentation of the gospel that distorts the concept of grace is a 'different gospel' (1:6). Even though Paul refers to a '*different*' gospel, in reality there cannot be '*another one*' (1:7). He will not credit multiple ways of salvation, or many roads to heaven, or a variety of ways to fellowship with God. Pluralism for Paul is out of the question. There is only one gospel and all other forms are perversions. For him there is no relative truth: what is true for me may not be true for you. Distortions from the way Paul understands the gospel, *from the way the gospel has been revealed by God*, are merely human and are examples of man's greatest crimes.

What is at stake here is more than a Christian view on alcohol, or fictional literature, or the propriety of head-coverings; *the gospel itself is at issue*. It is a matter of truth versus heresy. Paul speaks elsewhere of issues which are of first importance (*1 Cor.* 15:3) and, by implication, issues which are of secondary importance. The issue at Galatia was of the former category.

The language becomes darker and the accusations more vehement. Some are trying to '*trouble*' these Galatians; they want '*to distort*' the gospel, being '*contrary*' to everything Paul had expressed. There can be no appeasement, no reconciliation of views, no meeting of minds on this issue. And to make it clear once again, it is not so much that they were going against something Paul had said. That was true, but it was not the point. They were denying something of which Paul was merely the messenger – 'the delivery man'.

Paul employs a verb with technical associations: they had '*received*' what Paul had preached. Paul wrote about the Lord's Supper to the Corinthians, describing how he '*delivered*' to them what he had '*received*' from the Lord (*1 Cor.* 11:23). Paul was the 'messenger,' but the message was the Lord's. These Galatians had likewise initially '*received*' (1:9) from Paul that which he had delivered to them ('*the one we preached to you*' 1:8). In so doing they had acknowledged the message as coming from an authoritative source that transcended the apostle. Now they were turning their backs on it. And in reality they were turning their backs on God.

It is just here that Paul brings out his darkest threat of all.

## ANATHEMAS

Many in today's church regard Paul at this point as utterly opinionated and intolerant. What possible right or justification does he have to pronounce a curse on these false teachers in Galatia? Is this not the very height of arrogance and conceit on the apostle's part? It seems such an unloving gesture. No wonder he fell out with Barnabas and Peter! He was such a difficult man to get on with– always correct, always insistent upon his own view, intolerant, conceited, and judgemental.

But before we rush into hasty post-modern assessments of the apostle we need to slow down and examine why it is that he is saying this at all. Several things are worth noting:

1.  Paul is prepared to condemn *himself* for the same perversion of the gospel if he is found guilty of it. It is the gospel and not his own reputation that is at issue.

2.  Furthermore, the same would be true were an angel to proclaim something different. The truth of the gospel he proclaimed is *that* certain. No doubt some heavyweights in Galatia had weighed in, swaying the weak-minded to ambivalence over what once they had regarded as certain. Error is error no matter who speaks it.

3.  The precise word Paul uses at this point, '*accursed*' (twice, 1:8 and 1:9) is once more derived from Old Testament connotations of covenant and its violation. The equivalent word in the Hebrew of the Old Testament is *harem*, which is rendered 'devote to destruction' in Leviticus 27:28–29, Deuteronomy 7:26 and 13:17. It is vividly illustrated by the story of Achan in Joshua 6. Specific instructions were given with regard to the destruction of Jericho that 'the city and all that is within it shall be devoted to the Lord for *destruction*' (*Josh.* 6:17). Achan's violation of this rule brought upon him and his family the penalty of death. What he had failed to do, the devoting of these items to destruction, he himself must bear. He had violated covenantal obligations with regard to membership in the community of God.

Painful and shocking as that story is, Paul intends his Galatian readers to understand that the agitators among them must be handed over to destruction. What that means precisely is not spelled out here. Later (at 4:30) Paul may be suggesting that they be expelled from the church. Even here it is clear that it involves the shunning of their teaching.

Paul's words are in the form of a request (a prayer!) that *God* would curse them. Lest they misunderstand it, Paul repeats it for emphasis, reminding them ('*again*', 1:9) that this is what he had told them when he had been with them even though this issue had only been theoretical at that time. By now it is a very real problem and they must be keenly aware of it.

How can a Christian ever pray such a prayer? Are we not to love our enemies, bless those who curse us, judge not lest we be judged and forgive even as we are forgiven? Isn't this the very reason why some have long since abandoned Paul for Jesus, seeing in the teachings of Jesus an ethic far gentler and more spiritual than the vengeance that often seems to characterize the apostle? But such an antithesis between Jesus and Paul is a hallmark of false religion. The repudiation of the gospel of grace is a repudiation of Jesus. Any gospel that introduces anything other than the mercy of God in Jesus Christ as the cause of salvation, is a denial of God himself. It is to proclaim another authority in opposition to God's authority. And such a gospel will always eventually be condemned. Paul is not denying the possibility of repentance and forgiveness for individuals who may now be guilty of heresy. But he is asking God to vindicate his truth and uphold his integrity.

When a person denies the gospel, there is only one possible consequence: *condemnation*! There is no alternative. The gospel delivers us from condemnation (*John* 3:16), but without such a deliverance we will certainly be condemned. When a person rejects the gospel, the free, gracious gift of God's forgiveness and kingship, then he remains under the divine curse that is the inevitable reflex of God's holiness toward sin.

There is only one gospel. Indeed what was then being preached by some in Galatia was (literally) a 'bad-news-gospel' (1:8). The gospel has a shape that is certain and fixed. It brooks no tampering. Truth exists and truth matters. This is a message that is very much counter-cultural today. But Paul did not just smile at a perversion of the gospel and say, 'Whatever! Each to his own!' The gospel is not a matter of Paul's personal preferences. Rather, the word that comes from God is double-edged: a word of salvation and rescue for those who believe it; a word of condemnation for those who reject it or tamper with it.

# 3

# Conversion and Call

*For am I now seeking the approval of man, or of God? Or am I
trying to please man? If I were still trying to please man, I would
not be a servant of Christ.* <sup>11</sup> *For I would have you know, brothers, that the gospel that
was preached by me is not man's gospel.* <sup>12</sup> *For I did not receive
it from any man, nor was I taught it, but I received it through a
revelation of Jesus Christ.* <sup>13</sup> *For you have heard of my former
life in Judaism, how I persecuted the church of God violently
and tried to destroy it.* <sup>14</sup> *And I was advancing in Judaism beyond
many of my own age among my people, so extremely zealous was
I for the traditions of my fathers.* <sup>15</sup> *But when he who had set me
apart before I was born, and who called me by his grace,* <sup>16</sup> *was
pleased to reveal his Son to me, in order that I might preach him
among the Gentiles, I did not immediately consult with anyone;*
<sup>17</sup> *nor did I go up to Jerusalem to those who were apostles before
me, but I went away into Arabia, and returned again to
Damascus* (Gal.1:10–17).

The gloves are off! We are barely into the first chapter and already
Paul has prayed down curses on those in Galatia who were
advocating a 'different gospel' from the one he had proclaimed to
them. And even though Paul is aware of the different groups that
lie behind the problem in Galatia – and later he will imply that one
individual may be responsible more than any other - he is not
concerned about winning the approval of this party or that; his goal
is to be faithful to what God had disclosed to him. 'For I did not

receive it from any man, nor was I taught it, but I received it through a revelation of Jesus Christ' (1:12).

But wait a minute! Hasn't Paul said something like this already? Didn't he start the letter by saying, 'Paul, an apostle – not from men nor through man' (1:1)? Yes, there is a similarity, but he is not merely repeating himself. In the opening verse he is defending his apostleship, his credentials, his right to be heard. Here, in this section, he is defending the message he proclaimed, 'the gospel that was preached by me' (1:11). Obviously, the two things belong together: if Paul is not an apostle then what he has been preaching and teaching bears no authority, and the Galatians are not in any way bound to heed it.

## DEFENSIVENESS

A man's reputation can be important. But is Paul not overly concerned about his reputation here? Is he bordering on a self-justification that renders him open to the charge of egotism? Paul, we can hear some say, has too high an opinion of himself!

Jewish Christians, for example, might have been asking, 'What could someone who has abandoned the Jewish traditions possibly know about the way of salvation?' Accusations of Paul's treachery were prevalent among the Jewish diaspora. And in Gentile circles, things were no better. Paul had little history. He had come out of nowhere. Some were deeply suspicious of his motives. It was one thing for the likes of James or Peter or John to lecture them about error. They after all had spent time with Jesus. They knew him in a way that Paul did not. More than likely, some of Paul's accusers were applying the 'divide and conquer' rule, suggesting that the apostles of Jerusalem (men like James and Peter) were proclaiming a different (better!) version of the gospel. There is more to this charge than we might suspect, as we shall see later when we examine the second chapter of this letter.

These criticisms were powerful enough to utterly undo any claim made by the apostle. The truth is, however, that Paul was not claiming that his view, his opinion, was right, but that he was declaring the view given to him by God. Of course, every religious huckster in history has claimed as much. Why should Paul be any different? Isn't the retort, 'It's not what I say, but what God says', a little too simplistic? Paul may be assured of his role, but how could those in Galatia be sure of it?

The answer to this question is to apply the criterion of the apostle John: 'Beloved, do not believe every spirit, but test the spirits to see whether they are from God, for many false prophets have gone out into the world' (*1 John* 4:1). The church was to do exactly this with Paul and would concur that he really was who he claimed to be. However, the approval of Paul's claim given to him by the Church does not make it any easier for him here: in the letter to the Galatians Paul is treading virgin soil. And to some his words are so much hot air!

## DISTORTIONS

Why is Paul on the defensive anyway? The answer is that some 'want to distort the gospel of Christ' (verse 7). What exactly had they done to distort it? The precise answer to this question is what Galatians is all about, and we shall have to be patient before we discover the answer fully. However, there is a clue given to us in verse 11, where Paul insists that the gospel he had preached was 'not man's gospel.' This no doubt means the same as that suggested in the opening verse with regard to Paul's apostleship – that it did not *originate* with man. However, as marginal notes in some Bible translations will indicate, it may also mean that Paul's preaching of the gospel was *not according to man* in the sense that it did not pander to human desires. There is more than a hint in this letter that some in Galatia were adjusting the gospel, making it more palatable, less demanding, less *offensive*.

There have always been those who wish to lessen the demands of the cross of Christ. Paul will bring this charge to the full light of day in the closing section of the letter, stating as clearly as is possible that their motivation all along has been 'that they may not be persecuted for the cross of Christ' (6:12). There is a cost to remaining faithful to the gospel; it is the cost of true discipleship. The urge to lessen its demands is understandable but deadly. Paul does not want his readers to misunderstand the seriousness of doing so: those who meddle with the gospel will be cursed (1:8–9).

Already, a lesson emerges: *truth matters!* We are to be as concerned for the purity of the gospel as Paul was. If we find ourselves irritated by what we regard as nit-picking as we read these opening verses, then it is all too possible that a dangerous spirit has already overtaken us. We must be on our guard lest we attempt to modify the demands of the gospel to suit our own prejudices, or 'needs'. Error, more often than not, enters by a door named 'indifference'.

This may sound a little intimidating. Do I need to 'understand all mysteries' to ensure compliance here (see *1 Cor.* 13:2)? Thankfully not! We do not have to be expert apologists for the gospel, though we should strive to be the best we can with the talents God has given to us. Rather, it is a call to understand the basics, the *essentials* of the gospel. Have you ever noticed just how many times Paul says, 'I want you to *understand*' (see *Rom.* 11:25; *1 Cor.* 2:12; 11:3; 12:3; *Eph.* 5:17; *2 Tim.* 3:1)?

## FROM PERSECUTOR TO PREACHER

Paul mentions a 'former life' (1:13). Not every Christian has a conversion experience as radical and sudden as Paul; but every true Christian knows something of, what we might call, 'what I once was by nature' in contrast to 'what I am now by grace'.

Not every conversion is the same. Indeed, the details of our conversions are as personal and distinct as our DNA or fingerprints might be. Our former life may not be as bad as Saul's; and there again, it may be worse. The conversion may be sudden, or like a mother awakening her child from sleep – with a kiss! 'God breaketh not all hearts alike', says Richard Baxter.

Some, who have trusted in Christ since infancy, may not recall a 'former life'. But by nature each one of us is in union with Adam – something that has to change if we are to become Christians.

Several things now come to the surface:

1. Paul's past was not something of which to be proud. He had, as he now relates, 'persecuted the church of God violently and tried to destroy it' (1:13). Indeed, it sounds as though they had been mulling over this very thing in Galatia, since Paul prefaces it with the remark, 'For you have heard of my former life in Judaism.' One

imagines the apostle's enemies rubbing this in, encouraging a spirit of cynicism and distrust in his words. Paul relates in verses 22 and 23 that when he first arrived in the region of Galatia his reputation had gone before him. Better to be up front and open about this foul blemish in his past, for there were those ready to expose him as a hypocrite. Had there been daily newspapers, one could imagine a headline in the equivalent of the *Jerusalem Times*, or *Galatian Independent*, 'The Double Life of Saul of Tarsus'!

What an argument for inspiration this is! The Spirit led Paul openly to confess what he might otherwise have tried to conceal.

2. Paul's doubtful past made him an unlikely candidate for the work of chief apostle to the Gentiles. He was far from being 'open' to receiving this gospel from someone else, guided and motivated by human interests and promotion as he was. (This is the suggestion behind verse 11). On the contrary, Paul's hounding of Christians to their death (*Acts* 22:4; 26:9) made him the least likely advocate of Christianity to the frontiers of Europe. He had 'persecuted the church of God' after all! There was blood on his hands! Not a day would pass without Paul being reminded of his dreadful complicity in bigotry and persecution. The death of Stephen in particular was to have a profound effect upon Paul. It can be argued with some cogency that Paul's fondness for the expression 'in Christ' – it is in many ways his *signature* and he uses it over 160 times – was forged in his mind as he contemplated the fact that in persecuting Stephen and others he had actually been persecuting Jesus (*Acts* 7:54–8:1; 9:4–6)! Had the church wished to find a spokesman for emerging Christianity, it could have chosen better than Saul of Tarsus.

3. Paul was a zealous Pharisee. The language is very strong here. He speaks of 'advancing in Judaism' (1:14). This is a technical expression found only here in Paul's writings. Roughly speaking, the Jewish world of Paul's day could be divided between two communities. On the one hand, there were the 'liberals', known as (Seleucid) Hellenists. On the other hand, there was the stricter sect of Judaism, noted for allegiance to the Law (the *Torah*) and a patriotic allegiance to the nation of Israel.

Paul had belonged to this latter group. In words that reflect what he would later write to the Philippians, Paul outlines his Judaistic credentials (see *Phil.* 3:1–11). Nationalism – concern about racial purity and therefore a deep suspicion of the inclusion of proselyte Gentiles without strict regulations that ensured their full compliance with all Jewish 'markers' (Sabbath, table-fellowship and circumcision, 'the traditions of my fathers' [1:14]) – had marked his former life. He had attached great significance to law-keeping. Whatever the exact relationship between the gospel and these two issues (traditional identity markers and law-keeping), Paul wants his readers to understand his former advocacy of both. There is a sense in which Judaism (in its view of law and tradition) and the gospel are in opposition to each other. It is too early to ask in what way this is so. Paul is keeping this thunder for the second chapter. For now he wants us to understand that he has changed – changed so radically that he bore a different name.

4. The contrast between 'Judaism' and 'the church of God' (1:13) is worthy of some reflection. It is all too easy for us, two millennia later, to make this distinction, but in the middle of the first century, the church had barely begun to emerge as something distinguishable from its Jewish roots. The strategy had initially been to visit the synagogues in every town and city, a strategy that continued into the second and third missionary journeys (*Acts* 13:14–15; 13:43; 14:1; 17:1, 10, 17; 18:4, 7–8; 18:17, 19, 26; 19:8). Christians separated from the Temple and its sacrificial liturgy very quickly, but away from Jerusalem, the synagogue services had long since developed a momentum of their own. It was not difficult to avoid attending the sacred festivals in Jerusalem, particularly if one lived hundreds of miles away. It was another to separate from the local synagogue in the place where one lived.

Even though Paul now distances himself from Judaism, he still speaks of the Jews as 'my people' (1:14; 2:15). It is not yet clear in the middle of the first century what the 'church' will look like. That will take some time. A council in Jerusalem will help establish some very clear boundaries on certain issues (*Acts* 15:19–21), but not on every issue. Already, however, 'the church' is something very different from Judaism in Paul's mind. There is no meeting of minds here. It is a contrast and not a comparison. Paul is still a Jew, ethnically. Nothing can ever erase that. Paul, later, will distinguish between a person who is born a Jew and one who is one 'inwardly' (*Rom.* 2:29). And for the rest of his life, he will carry a deep burden for those whom he regards as 'my kinsmen according to the flesh' (*Rom.* 9:3).

## FROM JESUS TO PAUL

Paul is defending himself against the charge that he had been manipulated into proclaiming his gospel for ulterior motives. What exactly these suggested motives might have been is difficult to imagine. But he was certainly not motivated by any desire for financial gain or popularity.

Paul's response is to declare that he had received the gospel directly from Jesus! There had been no human intermediary who might have sullied things. The point? That if you dare to criticize this gospel, you are criticizing Jesus Christ himself!

A threefold account of Paul's conversion is now given in terms that are worth dissecting and examining closely.

1. Paul was 'set apart' before he was born (1:15). Before he was born – and Paul has in mind *long before*, in *eternity* – God had determined that Saul of Tarsus would be converted. This is the doctrine of predestination: that God determines beforehand what we are to become. Hated as that notion is by some, it is for Paul the assurance that what has taken place owes its origin to God himself and not to some (changeable) decision of the apostle. As an anonymous hymn writer puts it:

> *I sought the Lord, but afterward I knew,*
> *He moved my soul to seek him, seeking me.*

2. Though there was a determination by God in eternity to save the apostle, the way this is brought about (in human experience) is by a 'call': Paul was 'called by grace' (1:15). This is an effectual call that accomplishes what it solicits. According to a 'formula' that Paul would later enunciate, 'those whom he predestined he also called,

and those whom he called he also justified, and those whom he justified he also glorified' (*Rom.* 8:30). Paul is tracing the signature of God's handwriting all the way from eternity to the point where his soul concurred with the invitation to believe in Jesus Christ. At every point it was the Lord's doing.

3. In an amazing statement, Paul then describes how God revealed his Son 'to me' (1:16). Translations have taken many views of this phrase, rendering the preposition variously as 'through' or 'in'. Paul is saying something more than that he was now to be used as the instrument through which Christ was to be made known to others (as the word 'through' would suggest). He is underlining the fact again that he had seen Christ. This is best taken as a reference to the Damascus Road experience.

We know from the account of Paul's conversion in Acts that Jesus appeared to Paul – physically (*Acts* 9:5). 'Have I not seen Jesus our Lord?' he would ask the Corinthians (*1 Cor.* 9:1). But this does not exhaust Paul's meaning. Paul wants to say that he had come to know Jesus in more than just the physical sense – that of meeting him on the road to Damascus! He had come to know him in a way that convinced his heart of Christ's Lordship. He had seen with the eye of faith and had responded in worship. This monotheistic Jew had bowed the knee and worshipped Jesus.

What has emerged in this section is an argument defending Paul's preaching along the following lines of thought:

i. Paul was a most unlikely candidate to have been chosen to make the gospel known to the Gentiles

ii. His conversion had been by a sovereign work of God

iii. At the time of his conversion and for a period of three years afterwards, he was nowhere near Jerusalem.

If Paul was not anywhere near Jerusalem during this time, where was he? The answer is Arabia, but it is an answer that raises a host of questions as to the exact location. The mystery is made deeper because in Acts there is no mention of any visit to Arabia.

Some insist that this is the region of the Arabian Peninsula, perhaps Mount Sinai itself, and that Paul saw himself as another Moses. One contemporary author insists that Paul saw himself as another Elijah, though it is difficult on this score to see the connection with Mount Sinai. All of this seems unlikely. A better solution would be to note the account given in 2 Corinthians 11:32–33, where Paul mentions being tracked down by the governor of King Aretas in Damascus, presumably after Paul had returned from his visit to Arabia. Paul, it will be recalled escaped the city by being let down in a basket over the side of the city wall. This would make 'Arabia' equivalent to the region governed by King Aretas – the Nabatean kingdom.

This ancient kingdom of the Middle East was sited in present-day Jordan and had its capital at Petra. It was established in the late 4th century BC, and by 85 BC controlled the northern Red Sea coast, Damascus and Lebanon. Following the conquests of Pompey in the Levant in 63 BC, Nabatea became an ally of Rome. The kingdom was annexed by Trajan in 106 AD, becoming the Roman province of Arabia.

If difficulty exists in identifying the reference to Arabia, it exists also in ascertaining what Paul might have been doing in Arabia for up to three years (though it is not necessary for us to think that Paul spent the whole of those three years in Arabia). One imagines him spending time pouring over the Scriptures (the Old Testament) and formulating in his understanding his theological convictions. It is tempting to think of this period as the necessary period of reflection and study before his life's ministry of teaching and preaching – something akin to a modern seminary education.

Those who cavil at the need for such a preparatory period in 'school' need to reflect that Jesus did not begin his own public ministry until he was in his late twenties, after what had been many years in private contemplation and intense study of the things of God.

But the fact that Paul had evidently upset the Nabateans seems to imply that he had also preached there, disturbing them with what they saw as some errant branch of Messianic Judaism. It is hard to imagine Paul anywhere without some accompanying evangelism. Nabatea had proved an early training ground for missions. Here he had learned to taste the painful cost of discipleship. Here, in this region of the Roman Empire, he had been given a foretaste of things to come: 'through many tribulations we must enter the kingdom of God' (*Acts* 14:22).

# 4

## Fifteen Days with Peter

*Then after three years I went up to Jerusalem to visit Cephas and remained with him fifteen days. [19] But I saw none of the other apostles except James the Lord's brother. [20] (In what I am writing to you, before God, I do not lie!) [21] Then I went into the regions of Syria and Cilicia. [22] And I was still unknown in person to the churches of Judea that are in Christ. [23] They only were hearing it said, 'He who used to persecute us is now preaching the faith he once tried to destroy.' [24] And they glorified God because of me* (Gal. 1:18–24).

Paul is recalling past journeys. Following his conversion he went from Damascus to Arabia and back again. How long he was in Arabia we cannot be certain. Assuming that 'after three years' is a reference to his conversion, rather than after his return to Damascus, this would imply that Paul might have spent a considerable period of time in Arabia – long enough to get into trouble, as the incident involving King Aretas suggests. Now, he makes a trip to Jerusalem.

That Paul should visit Jerusalem is no great surprise. What is surprising is that it had taken this long for him to make the journey. Jerusalem was the focal point of emerging Christianity. It was where some of the chief apostles resided and worked. Everything about this visit suggested difficulties. Paul, after all, had been 'enemy number one' on the Jerusalem prayer list. And now he was coming to them as one who (in the estimation of some) had established himself as chief spokesman for Christianity!

Several things are worthy of note in regard to Paul's visit to Jerusalem.

## Fifteen Days with Peter (1:18–24)

1. Jerusalem remained at this point in history the centre of all things religious. Christianity was still in its infancy and was considered by many as rooted in some way in Judaism, with its headquarters in Jerusalem. Many of the principal leaders of the young Church, men like James (the Lord's brother) and Peter, were there, giving shape and voice to the distinctives of Christianity. Jerusalem was looked upon as the nerve-centre, for good or ill, and as yet the 'apostle to the Gentiles', as Paul was to be known, had not met the Jerusalem apostles. News of his conversion had no doubt reached them. Given his history, it was inevitable that some would be deeply suspicious even of his conversion to Christ, let alone of his claim to apostolic authority!

2. Meeting the apostles was always going to be a tricky business. Paul was never a shrinking violet – not in his 'former life' (1:13), and not as a Christian. As we shall see later, he confronted both Peter and irenic Barnabas over a matter of principle. Even those of us who admire Paul might have found him difficult to get on with. Men of principle always are. But this meeting had a sense of inevitability about it. Paul could put it off no longer. It is amazing, to put it mildly, that the meeting of Paul and Peter should be summarized so briefly, 'I went up to Jerusalem to visit Cephas and remained with him fifteen days' (verse 18)! A thousand questions come to mind, but it is not Paul's intention to address them in this letter.

We need to pause and reflect on this a little. Remember, Paul had never spent time with Jesus, apart from the Damascus Road incident. He had never heard anything Jesus had said, taught or preached. He was not privy to any of the many occasions when Jesus had taken the disciples aside and instructed them. He had not witnessed at first hand any of the miracles that disclosed Christ's glory. He had not been one of the twelve in the Upper Room. Nor had he seen the crucifixion or witnessed the resurrection.

It is reasonable to imagine that this fifteen-day meeting with Cephas (Peter) would have been filled with instruction and questions from both men. What exactly would they have spoken about for these two weeks? Perhaps Paul had yet to hear the promise that Jesus had made to Peter, *the Rock*, that he intended to build the church 'on this Rock' and that nothing would be able to withstand his sovereign determination to do so (see *Matt.* 16:18). Surely, that was something for Peter to relate and for Paul to learn!

Remember that Paul is trying to defend himself against the charge that he had not received this gospel from men (1:12), just as he had not received his apostolic credentials from men (1:1). He was more than just a lackey of the Jerusalem power base – and the suggestion being made in Galatia was that he was an unreliable lackey at that! The gospel had been given to him by Jesus Christ himself. It is not that Paul is speaking ill of the men in Jerusalem in any way; nor is he denying that he may have learned from them (and they from him). But his authority did not come from them. It came directly from Jesus Christ.

It is unnecessary to insist that Paul and Peter did not confer on the gospel. The point is that, even granting some intense discussion, it would be unreasonable for anyone to charge Paul with being a mere puppet of the men of Jerusalem after he had been so short a time with them.

Even so, we are bound to ask the question: what did they talk about? But some things are best kept secret!

## JAMES, THE LORD'S BROTHER

Verse 19 introduces another puzzle: Paul did not meet any of the other apostles, apart from James, the Lord's brother. There are several ways of understanding this statement.

1. Paul could be suggesting that he had met with James, the son of Alpheus (*Mark* 3:18), one of the twelve apostles (disciples), but about whose later life we know next to nothing. But that would mean that Paul's use of the phrase 'the Lord's brother' was a very general one indeed, not a reference to a sibling as the phrase naturally suggests.

2. Some have taken this statement to refer to James, the Lord's brother, with the sense 'I didn't see any apostles, only James.' That is, taking 'apostle' in the very strict sense of 'one of the twelve', James therefore not being one of them. But most commentators take the view that Paul intends to *include* rather than *exclude* James from the apostolic band, understanding 'apostle' in a broader sense. This

interpretation however would make it difficult for Paul to insist, as he does in the opening verse, that he (Paul) was an apostle in the strictest sense possible, if he is prepared to call James, the Lord's brother, an apostle.

3. As just noted, most take the view that Paul intends to *include* rather than *exclude* James from the apostolic band. Paul is using the term 'apostle' in a more general sense here, as it is often used in the rest of the New Testament. Thus Barnabas (*Acts* 14:4,14), Andronicus and Junias (*Rom.* 16:7), and Epaphroditus (*Phil.* 2:25), are each referred to as apostles. In any case, since Paul records a resurrection appearance of the Lord Jesus to James, this last point may well be redundant (*1 Cor.* 15:7).

Even so, it is still astonishing that Paul met with only two people in Jerusalem: Peter and James. If this were literally all, it might explain why he felt the need to protest that he was not lying about it (verse 20). But this would be an inadequate understanding. Paul did meet with others in Jerusalem, Barnabas for example (*Acts* 9:27). But he may well be suggesting that these other 'meetings' were secondary and not to be viewed as having the same degree of importance as the meetings with Peter and James.

Even so, the meeting with Barnabas was a treasured one. It was Barnabas, irenic character that he was, who 'introduced' Paul to Peter and James. The need for such an introduction is, in part, explained by the fact that Paul was almost entirely unknown to the apostles, apart from his dreadful past. He was not, at this period of time, the famous missionary and evangelist that he would become. It is more than likely that many of the believers in Jerusalem were still deeply suspicious of Paul's 'conversion', suspecting him perhaps of false motives. This is precisely what Luke records in Acts 9:26, 'And when he had come to Jerusalem, he attempted to join the disciples. And they were all afraid of him, for they did not believe that he was a disciple.'

## SYRIA, CILICIA

Following his visit to Jerusalem, Paul made a visit to Syria and Cilicia (1:21). Paul's home-town, Tarsus, was in this region. Acts 9 fills in some of the gaps here. Paul evidently moved about freely in Jerusalem, speaking boldly to its inhabitants about Jesus (*Acts* 9:28). Then came a plot to have him killed. It arose from the Hellenists (*Acts* 9:29). This was the second attempt on Paul's life in less than a month (the first being in Damascus, before coming down to Jerusalem, when the governor of King Aretas found him).

It is at this point that certain 'brothers' escorted Paul to Caesarea, on the Mediterranean coast, and 'sent him off to Tarsus' (*Acts* 9:30) – where he had come from! One wonders if they might have thought that this would be the last they would ever see or hear of Paul? But nothing could keep this man quiet, and though we do not know anything of Paul's activity in this region, we can be sure that it involved elements of teaching and preaching. How long was he to be there? In 2:1, Paul makes a reference to another visit to Jerusalem 'after fourteen years'. If this is understood as fourteen years *following his conversion*, this would make his stay in Syria and Cilicia approximately ten or eleven years.

We may summarize matters in this way:

| YEAR (AD) | EVENT |
|---|---|
| 30 | Jesus' resurrection |
| 33–35 | Paul's conversion / visit to Arabia / sojourn in Damascus (*Acts* 9:19-25; *Gal.* 1:17–18). This requires reading 'after many days' (*Acts* 9:23) as being the 'three years' of *Gal.* 1:18. |
| 35 | Paul's first post-conversion visit to Jerusalem (*Gal.* 1:18). |
| 35-45 | Paul's years in Cilicia, Syria and Antioch (*Gal.* 1.21-2.1; *Acts* 9:30; 11:25). |
| 46 | Paul's second post-conversion visit to Jerusalem (*Gal.* 2:1; *Acts* 11:30). |
| 46–48 | First Missionary Journey to Galatia. |

[It will be noted that we have assumed the 'second' visit to Jerusalem to correspond with an account of a visit to Jerusalem recorded in Acts 11 rather than the one recorded in Acts 15 (the

Jerusalem Council), or even a later visit. We will return to this when we examine the first verse of chapter 2.]

## REJOICING IN JUDEA

The churches in Judea knew nothing of Paul's personal ministry at this time. They did, of course, hear of the conversion of Saul of Tarsus – news that was by now some three years old – and they rejoiced in that conversion, giving praise to God (1:23–24). Luke summarizes the blessing in this way: 'So the church throughout all Judea and Galilee and Samaria had peace and was being built up. And walking in the fear of the Lord and in the comfort of the Holy Spirit, it multiplied' (*Acts* 9:31). The point of this might not be clear at first, but recall that very different conclusions were now being drawn, a decade and a half later, in Galatia. Those folk in Judea were rejoicing that Paul, a one-time persecutor of the church was now proclaiming the gospel (the same gospel, note) up there in Tarsus and its surroundings. The believers in Galatia should remember this and include it in their considerations.

We have reached the end of the first chapter and, so far, all that Paul has managed to do is to defend himself against false charges. He is, of course, preparing the ground for something crucial – the answer to the question: *What is the gospel?*

*That* is what is coming up next.

# 5

# *Preserving the Truth of the Gospel*

*Then after fourteen years I went up again to Jerusalem with Barnabas, taking Titus along with me. <sup>2</sup> I went up because of a revelation and set before them (though privately before those who seemed influential) the gospel that I proclaim among the Gentiles, in order to make sure I was not running or had not run in vain. <sup>3</sup> But even Titus, who was with me, was not forced to be circumcised, though he was a Greek. <sup>4</sup> Yet because of false brothers secretly brought in-who slipped in to spy out our freedom that we have in Christ Jesus, so that they might bring us into slavery- <sup>5</sup> to them we did not yield in submission even for a moment, so that the truth of the gospel might be preserved for you* (Gal. 2:1–5).

We are into the second chapter and Paul is still writing his introduction! Already, we sense something of the tension in the air in that Paul has taken so long to prepare the way for what he really wants to say.

Opponents of his ministry in Galatia (the Judaizers) have been calling into question his right to be heard. This has involved Paul in writing a lengthy defence of his apostolic credentials.

Why does Paul have to defend himself against the charge that he had learned his message in Jerusalem? What is so wrong with that? On the face of it, nothing at all! And one answer is simple enough, and has already been supplied: it was not true! However, there are more subtle nuances to this charge that Paul thinks need exploring. From one point of view, it would have made perfect sense had Paul learned his doctrine from the apostles in Jerusalem. Who better to teach him than those who had known Jesus best: men like Peter and James? But that might have opened Paul up to the charge that he had not learned it very well, that, particularly, his understanding of the relationship of law and gospel was lacking. Paul, for a start, was not insisting that the Gentiles be circumcised, and this provoked in those Jews sympathetic to the gospel a suspicion that Paul had misunderstood something that they regarded as inviolable. Since the Galatians were far away from Jerusalem, Paul's opponents could accuse Paul of almost anything and it would have been difficult for Paul to defend himself as an *accurate* representative of Jerusalem theology.

Paul's insistence that he had learned his gospel from Jesus himself cuts right across this accusation (1:1, 11). There is more to this than a mere personality struggle between Paul and the false leaders and teachers in Galatia. Note the 'one-upmanship' that might be suspected in the retort, 'I have seen Jesus whereas you have not'!

The mention of Titus brings the real issue to the surface. *Circumcision!* Paul's insistence that Titus (a Gentile) should *not* be circumcised was a test case. It conveniently highlighted how the gospel of the New Covenant related to the Jewish ceremonial law of the Old Covenant. For the apostle, as we shall see, this was the very heart of the issue: to insist on some act of ceremonial obedience *over and above faith in Jesus Christ* was an issue of the highest possible significance. This was no peripheral matter. Salvation itself was on the line!

We will return to this in a moment, but first we need to settle some issues of chronology again. Paul's time markers are a little confusing and interpreters of this letter have understood them in different ways.

Paul mentions two visits to Jerusalem: one, 'three years' after his conversion (1:18), and a second visit 'after fourteen years' (2:1), this time in response to 'a revelation' he received from God (2:2). *When exactly* did this second visit take place?

## PAUL'S SECOND VISIT – WHEN?

History can be a perplexing study – sorting out dates! Assuming that Paul's mention of 'after fourteen years' (2:1) means fourteen years after his conversion (rather than after his *first* visit to Jerusalem), dates this visit around the year 46 AD. In all likelihood this is the visit recorded in Acts 11:30 – *before* the missionary journey to Galatia. Some have strongly argued that this is not the case, identifying this second visit with the official visit to Jerusalem in Acts 15 – the occasion of the Jerusalem Council. This would imply that this second visit took place *after* the missionary journey to Galatia.

If this latter view is correct, something of considerable importance arises. The Jerusalem Council had dealt with the issue of Jewish ceremonial practices and their place within the New Covenant. True, the issue of circumcision had not been central. But the Council did talk about matters relating to food (an issue which will emerge here in Galatians). It would surely be a little strange if Paul did not mention this Council, or its conclusions, in addressing issues in Galatia – particularly since they seemed so enamoured of the Jerusalem apostles. That Paul does not make mention of it makes it more likely that this Council had not yet taken place and that the visit being referred to is the one in Acts 11. Even granting that some might be tempted to make too much of the Jerusalem Council, it is inconceivable that a resolution of that Council would not be referred to at every possible occasion.

## BARNABAS

Paul went up to Jerusalem with Barnabas. He mentions Barnabas's name in the opening verse of this chapter in such a way as to suggest that Barnabas was his senior *in Jerusalem* (see *Acts* 15:12). Outside Jerusalem, the order always seems to be Paul and Barnabas (*Acts* 13: 9, 13, 43; 15:22, 36 etc.).

Barnabas's given name was Joseph. He was a Levite. Because of his sanguine character, the apostles nicknamed him 'Barnabas' – which means, 'son of encouragement' (*Acts* 4:36). As we have already noted, Paul assumed leadership over Barnabas (except, perhaps, in Jerusalem), but there is no hint of jealousy when the names are suddenly switched from 'Barnabas and Saul' (*Acts* 13:1) to 'Paul and Barnabas' (*Acts* 13:43). It is Barnabas who stood up for John Mark, despite his failure on the field of missionary service. When John Mark had gone home in the middle of the first missionary journey, Paul found it difficult to take him again. It was Barnabas who decided to take the risk and encourage John Mark in useful service in Cyprus, despite some public disagreement with Paul (*Acts* 15:36–41). Every church should have at least one Barnabas!

Paul is not telling us everything here! We have already seen this in the way Paul described his visit to Peter and James in Jerusalem a decade earlier, telling us nothing of what they talked about!

According to the account in Acts 11, following a wave of persecution in Jerusalem in which Saul of Tarsus had been involved – and which culminated in the stoning of Stephen – many Christians left and went to various cities, including Antioch. The conversion of many Gentiles (*Acts* 11:20, where some versions have the incorrect 'Greek-speaking Jews') made the folk in Jerusalem very suspicious, particularly since they were not being asked to 'become Jews' first. As a result, Barnabas was sent up to Antioch to investigate matters (*Acts* 11:22).

They could not have sent a better man! Barnabas found evidence of a genuine work of God and encouraged them to continue serving God. Luke adds, by way of comment about Barnabas, 'he was a good man, full of the Holy Spirit and of faith. And a great many people were added to the Lord' (*Acts* 11:24). Barnabas's testimony resulted in even more conversions.

Then Luke records that Barnabas went off to Tarsus to look for Paul, bringing him back with him to Antioch (*Acts* 11:25). This would have been the second occasion that Paul and Barnabas met (*Acts* 9:27). And for a year Paul and Barnabas taught the church in Antioch, after which, according to one view, they made the visit to Jerusalem that Paul now speaks of here in Galatians 2.

The chronology would then be that when Barnabas found Paul in Tarsus, the latter had already been ministering in the region of Syria and Cilicia (1:21) for a decade or so, and he had known and worked with Barnabas for another year in Antioch *before* coming to Jerusalem for this second visit.

## TITUS

We are now getting to the real purpose of this letter. Everything so far has been preparation. The main issue has to do with Paul's understanding of the gospel and the place of obedience to the ceremonial law: issues like circumcision, table-fellowship and the Jewish Sabbath.

But what has this to do with Titus? *Everything!* Titus was a Gentile. He was also a Christian. And Jewish Christians in Antioch had accepted him. And more importantly, he was not circumcised! Once again, the New Testament can surprise us. Luke in Acts never mentions Titus! He is referred to by Paul in several places, most notably for his skill in administering the offering collected in the Gentile churches for the poor Christians in Jerusalem (*2 Cor.* 8:6, 16, 20; 12:18). The church in Antioch sent Paul, Barnabas (and Titus) down to Jerusalem with the offering. This would have been some five years after the events being recorded here in Galatians 2 (if we identify the 'second visit' with Acts 11).

And, of course, Paul wrote a letter addressed to Titus.

It was because of 'false brothers' (2:4) that the Jerusalem church found itself in some tension over Titus. Evidently some in the mother church at Jerusalem considered the idea of an uncircumcised Gentile claiming to be a follower of the faith of Abraham unacceptable. And the outcome of this pressure was that they insisted that Titus be circumcised (2:3). But Paul would have none of it. This was a line in the sand.

Some have tried to argue that though Paul insists that Titus was not circumcised 'under compulsion', he was nevertheless circumcised *willingly*. This is in part argued because at a later occasion, and in very different circumstances where no matter of principle was at stake, Timothy was circumcised in order to provide greater opportunities of work among the Jews (*Acts* 16:3). But this idea about Titus would make no sense at all. It would be doubly difficult for Paul to maintain his argument if, after all, Titus was circumcised, willingly or not.

This was a showdown that was going to occur no matter what. It was necessary also if a way forward was to be found in the relationship between Jewish and Gentile Christians. Things were being assumed that, as yet, had not received 'official' sanction. Titus was to become the catalyst for doctrinal advance in the fledgling church's understanding of the gospel and its implications. This issue of circumcision is the focal point of a discussion as to what is the essence of the gospel, the essence of salvation itself.

# CIRCUMCISION

Circumcision was, for the faithful in the Old Testament era, the sign and seal of the covenant of grace. It was more than just a Jewish identity-marker of race and privilege; it was indicative of promises made and kept by God. If any pious Jew in Old Testament times were to be asked what guarantee he had of the forgiveness of sins, he would make mention, in some way or other, of circumcision. Not that they were to trust in the mark in the flesh itself; rather, the mark, the cutting, pointed to something that God had said and promised: an imputed righteousness received by faith alone!

In Paul's maturest reflection on this, written just under a decade later, he states that circumcision for a believer (like Abraham) was 'a seal of the righteousness that he had by faith while he was still uncircumcised' (*Rom.* 4:11; see *Gen.* 17:10). True, some Jews (many Jews!) came to see circumcision in a different way, seeing it as a badge of national identity more than of spiritual privilege. They, Paul would reflect, were only Jews 'outwardly' and not 'inwardly' (*Rom.* 2:28–29).

Circumcision was as important to believing Jews in the Old Covenant as baptism is for Christians in the New Covenant. And Paul would draw the closest possible parallel between the two (*Rom.* 4:11; *Col.* 2:11). Neither circumcision nor baptism is to be viewed as a converting ritual (operating, as it is sometimes rendered, *ex opere operato*, 'from the work done'). But neither are they to be separated altogether from conversion and what it signifies. Indeed, they indicate *and promise* that whoever exercises faith in God's Word of promise shall be saved from all their sins.

But we do not live under the Old Covenant any more. And these Gentile converts felt no allegiance to Old Testament rituals which they regarded as belonging to some former era of God's administration of the gospel. Titus, as a Gentile, had not been circumcised. And seemingly, he had not felt any pressure to undergo this ritual. But some saw things very differently indeed, insisting that Gentiles like Titus be properly circumcised.

# INTERLOPERS

As we have already said, things are a little tense in this letter. Even Paul's grammar gets a little scratchy! Scholars point out that Paul is guilty of using a 'sentence fragment' in verse 4. Paul is a touch annoyed, and he lets it show. What has upset him? Spies! What seems to have happened is this:

1. Paul (together with Barnabas and Titus) had a 'private' meeting in Jerusalem (2:2) with:

2. 'influential' members of the Jerusalem church (2:2, 6). Who these were we can only surmise, but probably Peter, James and John, together, possibly, with some others.

3. Spies (in the plural!) were 'brought in' (2:4). This gives rise to several questions and comments:

i. Where did this occur? We are assuming that this took place in Jerusalem, though some have tried to suggest that Paul is talking about a meeting in Antioch *before* he went down to Jerusalem, and that therefore:

ii. the spies were in fact an official delegation sent by James and the others from Jerusalem. This is unlikely because James would have every right to inquire what was going on in Antioch, just as the folk in Antioch had every right to come down to Jerusalem and ask for a meeting. Even if the meeting is the private one in Jerusalem, we must still ask:

iii. Who sent them? Paul insists that they didn't come on their own initiative, but were 'brought in' (2:2). Did James or Peter or John do this?

iv. Paul doesn't mince words: these men were spies, interlopers, who had no business being there at all. This was underhand and treacherous. Is Paul accusing James or Peter or John (or all three) of this? Or was this due to someone else in the Jerusalem church other than these three pillars?

v. There is the outside possibility that these 'spies . . . secretly brought in' were in fact the ones causing trouble in Galatia, the ones described in 1:7 as troubling the church by preaching another gospel. Could it be that the Jerusalem church was so suspicious of the 'Gentile factor' that they were prepared to bring these men down and secretly bring them into this meeting? Paul will say that what he was doing in Jerusalem was on behalf of the Galatian brethren (2:5, 'for you').

vi. Paul refers to these spies as 'false brothers'. Does this mean he is prepared to regard them as 'brothers' even though their deed here is treacherous?

vii. Their intent is clear enough: they were trying to 'spy out our freedom . . . in Christ, so that they might bring us into slavery' (2:4). *Freedom*! Here is the word that could be the title for the entire letter. Paul is concerned to protect true Christian liberty. The gospel emancipates. It delivers us from the yoke of bondage and tyranny. It sets us free to be the kind of people God intends us to be.

We need to be particularly careful here for it is all too easy to make Paul say something which he is not in fact saying. Paul is *not* suggesting that the gospel delivers us from all and every necessity to obedience to the law. Far from it: obedience is the evidence of our justification, as we shall see later. But we are free from certain aspects of the law – the ceremonial aspect of the law that was fulfilled in Christ, for example, or religious laws which were of human origin rather than divine. Not for a moment would Paul accept that such laws had any further authority over believers. The word 'freedom' occurs in various forms a dozen times in the six chapters of Galatians, for example: 'For freedom Christ has set us free; stand firm therefore, and do not submit again to a yoke of slavery' (5:1). Not for a moment would Paul yield on what he regarded as a fundamental principle. To require circumcision now would compromise the gospel itself, a gospel which at its heart promised salvation by grace, without additional requirements of obedience on our part.

There is high drama here, and evidence of real tension between Paul and the men in Jerusalem. Whatever the exact details, we have here clear evidence that the Early Church experienced growing pains. Men of the highest spiritual calibre can disagree and be suspicious of each other (and with good and justifiable cause). It is easy for us to look back and be critical of one side or the other. But if we had been in Jerusalem, we too would probably have been suspicious of Paul, and if we had been one of Paul's travelling companions we would probably have been angry with the men in Jerusalem. Christian work requires the most intense patience and courage.

## A NEW PERSPECTIVE?

Recent studies in Paul (and therefore of the letter to the Galatians) have gone through what we might call a *volte-face*. This 'new perspective' insists that we have seriously misunderstood the nature of Paul's confrontation with Jewish factions in the New Testament, because we have seriously misrepresented the nature of Pharisaism and gospel opposition. This has, of course, serious implications for the way we understand Galatians. It is insisted that the letter was not written to counter a 'justification-by-works' – or effort-on-our-part – theology. This is the traditional interpretation. Rather, the entire focus of the Galatian letter was to argue the case that Gentiles are to be included in the church – that justification is God's declaration of covenant membership.

According to this 'new perspective' the issue becomes one of Jewish intolerance of Gentiles rather than of the answer to the question of how we may become right with God. The issue becomes one of church membership (*who may be considered as belonging?*) rather than one of salvation itself (*how may we be saved?*).

For Jewish *Christians*, circumcision continued to have a deep significance as a badge ('marker') of their national identity as Jews. Becoming Christians had not changed that. If Gentiles were now to be received *without circumcision*, this seriously undermined the identity of this new group. 'False brothers' (2:4), perhaps the very agitators in Galatia, had been smuggled into a private meeting in Jerusalem to hear what Paul was really up to. And what they found was deeply disturbing to them. Gentile Christians were being allowed into full covenant membership without any requirement for circumcision, the badge of their Christian-Jewishness.

To summarize: Is Paul's concern merely to point out to over-nationalistic Jews that Gentiles who trusted in Christ may also be considered full members of the covenant *without circumcision?* This is indeed a part of Paul's concern. But it is also true that Paul engages in an assault upon the Judaizers' understanding of the very nature of salvation itself. Something was wrong with the manner in which they understood *the way of salvation itself.* For Paul, the key concept was *justification* and the Judaizers' had failed to understand it. It was more than just the issue of *who* can be considered members of the covenant community; Paul detected in Galatia the deadly gravitational pull of a works-based religion. And it needed scotching.

# 6

## Paul, Peter and James

*And from those who seemed to be influential (what they were makes no difference to me; God shows no partiality)–those, I say, who seemed influential added nothing to me. [7] On the contrary, when they saw that I had been entrusted with the gospel to the uncircumcised, just as Peter had been entrusted with the gospel to the circumcised [8] (for he who worked through Peter for his apostolic ministry to the circumcised worked also through me for mine to the Gentiles), [9] and when James and Cephas and John, who seemed to be pillars, perceived the grace that was given to me, they gave the right hand of fellowship to Barnabas and me, that we should go to the Gentiles and they to the circumcised. [10] Only, they asked us to remember the poor, the very thing I was eager to do* (Gal. 2:6–10).

Things are a little tense in Jerusalem, as we have seen. It looks as if Paul was accusing James, Peter or John (or all three) of treacherous activity. This is not a chapter in the book, *How to Win Friends and Influence People*! Paul is distressed. Yes, Christians can show righteous anger.

Let us remind ourselves of what has happened. Paul (together with Barnabas and Titus) has arranged to meet with 'influential' leaders (James, Peter, John?) to discuss some matters. Whether Paul knew in advance that this meeting would focus on the question of Gentiles being 'forced' to undergo circumcision in order to be reckoned true Christians is not expressly mentioned. The fact that he took uncircumcised Titus along with him into the heartland of the early church suggests that Paul had some inkling of it all along.

Things have gone badly. Spies have infiltrated the meeting, sent no doubt by the 'false brothers' (2:4). Paul does not say so, but did the 'influential people' also secretly suspect Paul's soundness? True, they came around eventually to Paul's viewpoint (2:9), but were they initially sceptical enough to turn a blind eye to the antics of the 'false brothers'? Church politics often smells rotten, and Paul seems to be saying as much when he makes an otherwise unnecessary remark to the effect that, influential or not, it made no difference to him (2:6). Paul was never a man to be intimidated by rank. And neither is God; he 'shows no partiality' (2:6). We can almost feel the tension!

The Jerusalem apostles were men of considerable influence and reputation in both Jerusalem and Galatia. Paul wants the Galatians to understand that the Jerusalem apostles, despite what may have been initial misgivings, did not disagree with him! He uses the present tense – he needs his readers to understand that what he is about to say comes with the approval of the powerful men of Jerusalem as much as his own. The agitators in Galatia were no doubt citing the men in Jerusalem over against Paul. But he wants them to know that in the end they were agreed as to the nature of the gospel.

In the next chapter, in an incident that occurred back in Antioch, there appears to have been something of a setback when some of these men from Jerusalem refused to eat with Gentile Christians. No doubt the agitators in Galatia were making much of the occasion. But Paul will be blunt about it: it had nothing to do with principle and everything to do with cowardice and hypocrisy. More of that later. For now, it is important for everyone to understand that, in principle at least, they had all been of one mind in Jerusalem.

## IN THE COMPANY OF GREATNESS

Jerusalem had agreed with Paul that neither Titus, nor the Gentiles generally, were under any obligation to be circumcised for them to be accepted by God. Nor should they feel any obligation to submit to this procedure in order to be acceptable to Jewish-Christian scruples. It was not the Gentile Christians that needed a change of heart on this issue but Jewish-Christians.

What accounted for this agreement with Paul by the men of Jerusalem?

1. If the visit to Jerusalem referred to here is the one mentioned in Acts 15, then there would have been plenty of evidence of what God had accomplished through Paul from the success of the First Missionary Journey to Cyprus and the region of Galatia. It would be difficult to deny Paul his point of view in that the very existence of the Galatian Church came about through his instrumentality!

However, if we take the earlier date of Acts 11 (*before* the First Missionary Journey), the issue of trusting Paul's judgement would have been more difficult for them, and it is a mark of the great esteem in which they held him that they were willing to accept his point of view with so little evidence of his preaching and theological abilities.

Taking this latter view, it would have been fourteen years since Paul's conversion. Since that time he had been to Arabia for 'three years' and for the past decade had been in the region of Syria and Cilicia. While it would be interesting to imagine Paul spending this time in contemplation and study (and no doubt there must have been plenty of that), he was also preaching the gospel. We are not told in the description of Barnabas's visit to Tarsus, looking for Paul, that many converts were found there, but it would be hard to imagine that there were none (*Acts* 11:25). However, when he returned to Antioch, the blessing of God rested upon his (and Barnabas') ministry: 'For a whole year they met with the church and taught a great many people' (*Acts* 11:26). In one way or another, Barnabas may have been the chief cause of Paul's acceptance in Jerusalem.

2. The men in Jerusalem noted in particular that Paul had been entrusted with preaching the gospel *to the Gentiles*, just as Peter had been entrusted with preaching 'to the circumcised' (that is, to Jews, 2:8). Paul is not, of course, suggesting that there are two different gospels, one carefully tailored for Gentiles and another for Jews! Appealing as that may sound to post-modern ears, Paul has already emphatically stated that there is no other gospel other than the one he preached (1:7). Even though he has used the expression 'different gospel' (1:6), in reality it was no gospel at all.

Why then does Paul open up the possibility of such an interpretation by using these expressions, 'gospel to the uncircumcised' and 'gospel to the circumcised'? Some have argued, simplistically, that Peter was still preaching a gospel of law while Paul was now preaching a gospel of grace. In fact, Paul is not arguing here for a distinction about *what* was preached, but about those *to whom* the one gospel was being preached. Uppermost in view here are the different audiences to which Paul and Peter were preaching – not different messages. God equips workers so that they are suited for particular spheres of ministry. Paul makes it clear that he holds Peter and his ministry in the highest respect (2:8). This is important since Paul is about to say something scathing about Peter and Barnabas in the light of something that happened later (2:11–13).

## PILLARS

Three 'pillars' of the New Testament church were to be found in Jerusalem: Peter (his Greek name *Cephas* is used in 1:18 and 2:9), James and John. Imagine meeting all three of them on a visit to the city! Paul had first met Peter and James a decade earlier on his first visit to Jerusalem. Paul, Barnabas and Titus had been conferring privately with James – 'the Lord's brother' (1:19), John – the disciple 'whom Jesus loved' ( *John* 13:23; 20:2; 21:7, 20) and Peter – 'the Rock' (*Matt.* 16:18).

Is Paul's use of the term 'pillar' to describe these three men sarcastic? Shakespeare has Mark Anthony repeat, 'For Brutus is an honourable man', over the slain body of Julius Caesar. The more he repeats the phrase, the less honourable Brutus becomes in the crowd's estimation. Paul uses the word 'seems' four times in his description:

'those who *seemed* influential' (2:2)
'those who *seemed* to be influential' (twice in 2:6)
'*seemed* to be pillars' (2:9)

Some of these men, men like James, John and Peter, had known Jesus personally, 'in the flesh', as we say – something which Paul could never claim. Imagine them discussing some finer point of the gospel, and one of these three men interrupting Paul in mid-sentence saying, 'I can remember Jesus saying to me one evening as we walked by the shore of the Sea of Galilee . . .' What could Paul possibly say to counter that? These men *were* influential! Ask anyone in the church at Jerusalem what he thought of these men and the answer would be clear! James, the Lord's brother, had also now nailed his colours to the mast and confessed Jesus as Lord (see also *James* 1:1). Indeed, the Jerusalem church would honour him for many years to come as the one who had known Jesus in a way that none of the other apostles could match: a genetic connection!

Understandable as it may be for us to hear a note of sarcasm in Paul's ascription of their importance, it is surely unlikely that this was intended. Paul now adds a term that has passed into popular English idiom: these men seemed to be *pillars*. We talk about certain people being 'pillars of the community.' The original Solomonic temple in Jerusalem had two great pillars (called Jachin and Boaz). Did this ascription to these men as 'pillars' arise because the Church was beginning to be seen as the new temple of God (*1 Cor.* 3:16; 6:19; *Eph.* 2:21)? Perhaps Paul is expressing a sense of awe at the genuine respect in which these apostles were being held, greater respect than he had thus far received from any quarter, or as it happens, would receive throughout his entire life's ministry!

## THE RIGHT HAND OF FELLOWSHIP

The point of the apostle's historical recollection is to underline the sense of unity that emerged from this meeting in Jerusalem. All those who mattered in any way were in agreement – perfect agreement – on this issue. Paul has been determined to demonstrate that he was not in the pocket of any individual or pressure group. God had 'worked through me' – this was the point he wished to make.

It would be difficult to underestimate the importance of this point in the unfolding of the history of the early church. When Paul and Barnabas were given the 'right hand of fellowship' (2:9), something of the greatest importance was established in the minds of the leaders of the Early Church: that there was only *one* gospel, and even though there might be continuing differences of style and appropriate emphases, on the fundamental nature of the gospel there was complete accord. There was not to be one gospel for the Jews and another for the Gentiles. To whatever parts of the world Paul and Peter might now go in pursuit of their calling, one thing was understood: they went with the same message of salvation. And, more surprisingly for some, agreement had been reached over the status and meaning of circumcision.

It is one thing to agree a principle in a meeting of this sort; quite another to put it into practice in the face of pressure groups threatening dissolution of membership in a given community. Things seem on a high plane here, but shortly we shall see matters unravel in a potentially catastrophic way.


## THE POOR ARE ALWAYS WITH US

The section ends with one other item of agreement between Paul and the Jerusalem 'pillars': he and Barnabas were to 'remember the poor' (2:10). This was an issue Paul felt personally attached to. It was to be an issue that would continually concern the church of the New Testament. In particular, as it happened, that concern would be directed towards the folk at Jerusalem since it was there that poverty was to be felt most severely (see *Rom.* 15:26).

Recognition of the seriousness of this issue has been troublesome for the church in all ages. Today, materialism is the single biggest competitor with authentic Christianity for the hearts and souls of millions in our world, including many in the visible church. It is instructive that the early church did not attempt large-scale relief measures in order to meet this issue. Instead it resolved to engage in deeds of mercy that were within its ability to accomplish.

The New Testament does not contain a detailed list of acceptable items to own, vocations to practise, or percentages of income to be donated. C. S. Lewis may be wise in suggesting that the only safe rule is to give more than we can spare; our charities should pinch and hamper us. Our standard of living, our whole lives, must be informed by love. And when it comes to the poor *in our midst* we must adopt the same rule of thumb as the apostles: practical caring must be a priority.

# 7

## The Clash of the Titans

*But when Cephas came to Antioch, I opposed him to his face,
because he stood condemned. [12] For before certain men came from
James, he was eating with the Gentiles; but when they came he
drew back and separated himself, fearing the circumcision party.
[13] And the rest of the Jews acted hypocritically along with him,
so that even Barnabas was led astray by their hypocrisy. [14] But
when I saw that their conduct was not in step with the truth of
the gospel, I said to Cephas before them all, 'If you, though a
Jew, live like a Gentile and not like a Jew, how can you force
the Gentiles to live like Jews?'* (Gal. 2:11–14 ).

'Here he hath no trifling matter in hand, but the chiefest article
of all Christian doctrine. The utility and majesty whereof
whoso understandeth, to him all other things shall seem but nothing
worth. What is Peter? What is Paul? What is an angel from heaven?
What are all creatures together, to the article of justification, which
Paul saw in danger by the conduct of Peter?'

Thus wrote Martin Luther in his commentary on Galatians 2:11.
There could hardly be anything more important than what is being
discussed here!

We have sensed something of a tension from the very beginning
of the letter, but it is only now that we come to the heart of the epistle
– the real issue that Paul is going to deal with. The meeting in
Jerusalem between Paul, Barnabas and Titus on the one side and
James, Peter and John on the other had all the makings of a disaster.
Things *could have* gone terribly wrong. Whoever introduced 'spies'

into this private meeting was planning trouble. But God intervened, and for that we should ever be grateful. The meeting, which could have split the Church in two, ended with complete accord. Whatever form the 'right hand of fellowship' took (2:9), it was a demonstration of unity on the gospel message and confidence in Paul as an apostle 'to the Gentiles.'

Perhaps they parted with words like, 'Why don't you all come up to Antioch and visit us?' Sometimes we regret the invitations we give! The reciprocal meeting could not have been more disastrous. Whatever tension they managed to avoid on their visit to Jerusalem, the return visit to Antioch went horribly wrong.

The wrong itself seems to have been of Peter's doing. Nor was it done in private (as the meeting in Jerusalem had been). It was very public, and the consequence was very dramatic. This may suggest that Paul was not expecting it and therefore had in no way prepared for it. Paul and Peter had what we might call a 'face-off'. What could possibly have happened to bring about such a public display of disagreement and discord? To answer that question, we first of all need to unearth some background material concerning the social relationships and mores of first-century Judea.

Jews did not associate publicly with Gentiles, particularly when it came to eating. These issues did not play any significant part in the predominantly Jewish Jerusalem, but in Antioch things were different. Antioch was more cosmopolitan. True, the church did have the pressures of Pharisaical and Zealot forces critical of those Jews who, having become Christians, were forsaking their Jewish customs and laws. True, the churches in Antioch had much more of a Gentile constituency than the church in Jerusalem. Something of the 'Jewishness' of the church was being lost at Antioch, mainly because its members owed little or no allegiance to Jewish history and tradition. And the spark ignited over table-fellowship.

## PORK AND BLOOD

Jews (*and* Jewish Christians in this early period) had 'issues' with certain foods: pork, meat that had been offered to idols, and meat from which blood had not been sufficiently drained. These were more than just personal tastes (Do I like my steak rare, medium-rare, or well-done?). It was a matter of obedience to Jewish law. It was what Moses had stipulated in the Torah (*Lev.* 3:17; 7:26–27; 17:10–14).

Meat offered to idols needs some further explanation. Many religious rituals in the Gentile world involved the sacrifice of animals and a ritual of blood-shedding and offering. Much of the meat was still usable, and in societies where food provision was not plentiful, it was sold as food in the local market. Often, it was cheaper. Some learned 'to ask no questions for conscience' sake' and simply purchased, cooked, and ate the meat.

But sensitive souls, knowing that it had been offered to some pagan deity just a few hours previously, were unsure as to whether eating such meat involved participation in the pagan rite and therefore in some form of idolatry. The church would deal with this issue later in Corinth (*1 Cor.* 8). The issue rarely came up in Jerusalem. In Antioch, however, it was unavoidable.

These matters may be hard for us to comprehend, but for first-century Jews, they were of immense importance. The account of one of the greatest 'heroes' of the faith, Daniel, taking his stand against violation of food laws was the stuff of children's bedtime stories. Such a response had become definitive of what it meant to be Jewish, and Jewish-Christians were loth to discard this heritage. Furthermore, many Jews had lost their lives during the Maccabean revolt (167– 164 BC) when attempts were made to Hellenize them. The Pharisees in Jerusalem had made the issue even more important by forbidding Jews to eat at the same table (or within close proximity) to Gentiles. The issue had acquired social and cultural status further complicating the matter.

There are examples of behaviour which immediately mark us out as Christians – we may think in our own times of how certain Christians have held strict views on attending places of entertainment or on imbibing alcohol. For Jewish-Christians in Antioch, it was *food*!

## UNROCK-LIKE BEHAVIOUR

We are not told how soon after the return of Paul and Barnabas to Antioch (some 300 miles north of Jerusalem) this next incident occurred. In part, our ability to date it depends on our dating of the 'second visit' to Jerusalem. The precise answer to this chronological question is difficult, but what is certain is that Peter made a trip north to Antioch.

Peter is referred to by his Greek name Cephas (as in verses 9 and 14). Is this because his behaviour resembled his pre-conversion nature? Verse 12 will suggest that sometime later, 'certain men from James' joined him. Peter had been in Antioch for some time before being joined by the others, long enough for him to establish a pattern of 'eating with the Gentiles' (2:12). Then things went horribly wrong.

It is difficult to exaggerate the importance of the event that now follows. The 'apostle to the Gentiles' and the 'apostle to the Jews' have a very public clash in which one accuses the other of the most flagrant hypocrisy! Imagine a meal. Paul goes up to Peter, the two standing face to face. Serious words are spoken in raised voices. Everyone has stopped eating and there is silence. The aroma of cooked pork is perhaps in the air. Was it that Peter had objected to the food as such, or simply to those who were eating it?

It was not just Peter who had given offence. Barnabas too had yielded to the pressure of the situation and refused to sit at the same table as the Gentile believers. Paul's companion and right-hand man had publicly gone over to the other side! It was no longer an issue that could have been labelled 'Antioch versus Jerusalem', or 'Progressive Church versus Traditional Church'. It was now Paul *contra mundum* ('against the world'). Paul was alone.

Paul's reaction is instantaneous. He accuses both Peter *and* Barnabas of 'not walking in step with' the truth of the gospel (2:14). There is more at stake here than table manners. The gospel is being compromised. By doing what they did, Peter and Barnabas were indicating that the Gentile Christians in Antioch were deficient in some way, were not true brothers! Since he will later describe a Christian as one who 'walks in step with the (Holy) Spirit' (5:25), Paul is clearly signalling their behaviour as *unchristian* and out of accord with the mind of the Holy Spirit!

We can only guess at the private thoughts of these three men. But a theological principle was at issue for Paul, one that could not be ignored, or even dealt with privately. What was it?

When Peter first came to Antioch, he evidently did something that he probably would never have done in Jerusalem. He ate with

Gentiles! Jews regarded Gentiles as ceremonially unclean. Eating at the same table with them was out of the question, it involved ceremonial defilement of immense proportions and consequences.

Peter had, however, received a significant vision sometime before, in the seaside town of Joppa. He had been shown 'something like a great sheet descending, being let down by its four corners to the earth. In it were all kinds of animals and reptiles and birds of the air.' In this vision, Peter was told to 'rise . . . kill and eat' – eat, that is, as food, animals which had been regarded as unclean, which God's law (Torah) had declared unclean (*Acts* 10:11–13). The urgency of the vision lay in the fact that Peter was about to be invited to visit a Gentile Roman centurion named Cornelius, based at the headquarters of the Roman forces of occupation at Caesarea, some thirty miles to the north. There he would not only speak with him but eat at the same table with him as a guest (*Acts* 11:3), just as Cornelius's men had done with Peter in Joppa (*Acts* 10:23).

Peter had faced the ire of Jerusalem over this very practice in Caesarea: 'The circumcision party criticized him, saying, "You went to uncircumcised men and ate with them."' (*Acts* 11:2–3). Perhaps he still smarted from that rebuke and was not keen to experience it again. But at that time Peter had evidently stood firm on *this* very issue.

## CAPITULATION

Several things need to be disentangled here:

1. 'Some men' arrived from Jerusalem. They are described as 'from James', which adds to the problem. James was not in Antioch, but he might as well have been. James, the Lord's brother, had become the leading figure in the church in Jerusalem – perhaps in the church generally at this time. It is not difficult to appreciate the reason why this is so. Who better to tell about Jesus than his brother!

2. It is possible that these men were the very same ones that had been labelled 'spies' by Paul following their discovery at the 'private' meeting in Jerusalem. It is also possible that they were actually from Galatia and were the very ones who later had caused problems there

and had necessitated Paul's writing of this letter. This is the worst-case scenario. If this is true, things were very tense indeed between James and Paul, and the 'right hand of fellowship' that had been given on Paul's departure from Jerusalem was insincere.

3. James will later (how much later depends on the dating of that 'second visit' again!) write from Jerusalem of 'some persons' having 'gone out from us and troubled you with words, unsettling your minds, although we gave them no instructions' (*Acts* 15:24). Of course, this might be a reference to an entirely different group of 'persons'.

4. These 'men from James' were, then, claiming to represent him. Perhaps it was because they implied that their views represented those of James that Peter capitulated to their pressure. Even if James had not sanctioned them, Peter seems to have drawn the conclusion that their opinion mattered, and mattered greatly. Perhaps they were closer to James's true mind on this matter than he was willing to let be known.

5. Or was it that Peter was just afraid of these men because he was weak and prone to be fearful of any pressure group? He knew that James did not hold these views, but he was afraid of what might happen to him once he returned again to Jerusalem. Or was it his family that he was concerned about? It was one thing for him to make a stand, but his family and friends would suffer the consequences too.

6. What makes it plausible that something more than just cowardice on Peter's part is afoot is the defection of Barnabas. It is one thing to engage in psychological interpretations based on the vacillating character of Peter – the one who had failed to stand firm during Jesus' arrest and trial. It is another matter altogether for Barnabas to defect as well. It was Barnabas who had gone to Tarsus in search of Paul in the first place (*Acts* 11:25). It was Barnabas that Paul had taken with him to Jerusalem in order to introduce Titus to the men, knowing him to be an uncircumcised Gentile Christian and that this might spark a confrontation (which it did!). Paul's trust in

Barnabas was crucial to his acceptance by the men in Jerusalem at the private meeting. The fact that *he* could defect on this issue must have come as a staggering blow to Paul on every level, and we sense it in his words, '*even* Barnabas' (2:13). Did some lingering residue of mistrust remain between these two men? When Paul was contemplating a return visit to Galatia (the Second Missionary Journey), he and Barnabas separated over whether or not to take John Mark with them, an occasion that Luke describes as a 'sharp disagreement' (*Acts* 15:39). Some things are best not described in detail.

All of this provides a fascinating glimpse into the personalities of the early church, particularly Peter, Barnabas and, possibly, James. They were not free from sinful behaviour. Whichever way we interpret these passages in Galatians and Acts, these men were not spotless. Great leaders can sin too.

## PUBLIC CLASHES

Why did this clash have to be so public? Why did Paul see this as a defection from the truth of the gospel?

We may assume that Paul had remonstrated with Peter *privately* according to Jesus' instruction (*Matt.* 18:15–20). If so, this only further exacerbates Peter's stubbornness or cowardice or both. Since the incident was public (Peter's refusal to sit at the same table as Gentile Christians), the rebuke (and expected repentance) was equally public.

Peter's action implied that the Gentile Christians were not truly members of the household of faith – not according to the definition interpreted by 'the men from James'. Their uncircumcised status disqualified them. Though it may appear as though the issue here is food and kosher laws, the real issue is the fact that these professing Christians were Gentiles. As Acts 15:1 makes clear, the real issue was this: 'some men came . . . and were teaching the brothers, "Unless you are circumcised according to the custom of Moses, you cannot be saved"' (*Acts* 15:1). The Jerusalem Council of Acts 15 argued for restraint in eating certain things when others of a sensitive conscience were present, and Paul himself will make similar statements when he writes to the Corinthians (*1 Cor.* 8). Paul will even have Timothy

[52]

(the child of a mixed Gentile-Jewish marriage) circumcised, after arguing that Titus need not be! But when there are those who are *insisting* that without observance of the food laws, or circumcision, men and women *cannot be saved*, Paul must stand his ground and insist that the very gospel is at stake. This is more than the question of whether Gentiles are included in the church. Much more! It is the very essence of the gospel itself: justification by faith alone in Jesus Christ alone, *apart from the works of the law* (2:16; see *Rom.* 3:28). Do we have to live 'like Jews' in order to be saved? *That* is the real issue. And that raises the question of the nature of justification before God.

Neither Peter nor Barnabas were denying the gospel verbally. But their actions were calling it into question. By their inconsistency, by going back on what they had already practised before this time, they were undoing the validity of their own testimony and wounding the understanding of others as to the nature of the gospel. Segregation based on race does that *now* just as much as it did *then*.

But we run ahead of ourselves. Paul is now ready to tell us the real reason why he is writing this letter to Galatia!

And it is more than whether the menu is pork or beef!

Who won this battle in Antioch? Paul does not say, and that perhaps speaks volumes! It would certainly have been advantageous for Paul to now add, 'and Peter acknowledged the grievous error of his ways'. The fact that Paul does not do so suggests that things were uncertain, and that the clash of the titans had not produced a clear victor. He must have penned this letter to Galatia uncertain of what would occur on his visit to Jerusalem and the Council. We can now read Peter's two later New Testament letters and see that he has the greatest respect for Paul (even if he does think the apostle can write some things which are difficult to understand, *2 Pet.* 3:16!).

There is no major rift between Paul and Peter over the content *or shape* of the gospel. None! But at this point in history, this is not clear.

# 8

## *Justification by Faith or Law?*

*We ourselves are Jews by birth and not Gentile sinners;* [16] *yet we know that a person is not justified by works of the law but through faith in Jesus Christ, so we also have believed in Christ Jesus, in order to be justified by faith in Christ and not by works of the law, because by works of the law no one will be justified.*

[17] *But if, in our endeavour to be justified in Christ, we too were found to be sinners, is Christ then a servant of sin? Certainly not!* [18] *For if I rebuild what I tore down, I prove myself to be a transgressor.* [19] *For through the law I died to the law, so that I might live to God. I have been crucified with Christ.* [20] *It is no longer I who live, but Christ who lives in me. And the life I now live in the flesh I live by faith in the Son of God, who loved me and gave himself for me.* [21] *I do not nullify the grace of God, for if justification were through the law, then Christ died for no purpose* (Gal. 2:15–21).

We have come to the heart of the letter, the real reason Paul had written it. We can imagine its first readers being shocked by the tone of the first thirty-eight verses. And as for the section immediately preceding this one, where Paul explains his public opposition to the action of Peter, no doubt some of the Galatians may have heard a version of it *before* this letter ever arrived. Since Paul does not express what the outcome of it was, it is not unrealistic to imagine that there were Jewish-Christians in Galatia who were on 'Peter's side' on this issue – whatever that may have actually meant for them in Galatia. Given the degree to which Paul has been defending his authority as an apostle, that seems an altogether likely scenario.

But are we done with history? Perhaps not! The NIV places this entire section (2:15–21) in quotation marks, suggesting that this is something Paul told Peter in Antioch as he confronted him to his face.

Should Gentile Christians be more Jewish than they evidently were in accepting the (Jewish) Messiah? The refusal by Peter and Barnabas to engage in table-fellowship in Antioch signalled more than cowardice in the face of pressure tactics from Jerusalem; it suggested a deep-seated inconsistency in their understanding of the implications of the gospel of grace in Jesus Christ. They had shaken hands on it in Jerusalem following Paul's visit, but they had not worked out its consequences.

The fact that Paul had 'sided' with the Gentiles in opposition to Peter and Barnabas, made him open to all kinds of charges, one being that he didn't understand the depth of Jewish feeling on these issues. This he confronts head-on, with the dismissal that it deserves: 'We ourselves are Jews by birth and not Gentile sinners' (2:15). Paul knew more than most what Jews think!

Having established that point, Paul now comes to the crucial statement: 'yet we know that a person is not justified by works of the law but through faith in Jesus Christ, so we also have believed in Christ Jesus, in order to be justified by faith in Christ and not by works of the law, because by works of the law no one will be justified' (2:16).

## JUSTIFICATION

Recent studies in the writings of Paul have suggested that his pronouncements on justification have been misunderstood. According to this 'new perspective', Paul is only interested in the identity of those who belong to the kingdom of God and not with the answer to the question, 'How does someone become a member of this kingdom?' Paul's concern according to this view is to insist that Gentiles who believe in Jesus belong to this kingdom, just as much as believing Jews. This is something which folk like Peter and the others at Antioch were calling into question by their refusal to eat at the same table with Gentiles.

This is a central issue in the letter. Paul *is* concerned to include Gentiles in the kingdom over against Jewish-Christian prejudice. But is it not also true that Paul is concerned to answer the question, '*How is either a Jew or a Gentile saved?*' Is it by faith *alone* in Jesus Christ *alone*? Or is it a combination of faith *and* some qualifying work on our part? Is he not expressing his denial of any attempt to bring in the idea that we can 'add' to the work of Christ by insisting upon certain observances in order to salvation? What exactly does he mean by the expression, 'works of the law' as employed here (2:16)?

The idea that Paul is not concerned to ask (and answer) the question of *how a person gains admission into the kingdom of God* is ill-judged. For one thing, Paul seems to be engaging in deliberate contrasts in this section, not the least of which is the contrast between 'justified by faith' and 'justified by the works of the law' in verse 16. Recent studies deny this by insisting that the traditional viewpoint has also misunderstood the nature of Paul's use of justification!

Recall what Paul says. He begins, as we have seen, by insisting on his Jewish credentials. Why? Partly because some may be suspecting him of not understanding his Jewish brethren in Antioch. But this is not the main reason for doing so. Paul wants to underline the privileges associated with being a Jew. Note the (otherwise) distinctly uncomplimentary expression, 'Gentile sinners' (1:15)! Jews were sinners too, as Paul well knew ('all have sinned and fall short of the glory of God' (*Rom.* 3:23)). But here he is identifying for a moment with his Jewish-Christian brothers in acknowledging the advantages that are theirs by having been born and raised as Jews. Yet, for all that, 'the works of the law' could not justify him. What does Paul mean by this?

The phrase 'works of the law' occurs six times in Galatians, and twice in Romans (three times in some versions).

The 'new perspective' commentators have argued that by 'works of the law' Paul means such things as circumcision and the observance of food laws. Whilst Jews, too, are sinners, they have been the recipients of immense privileges: 'to them belong the adoption, the glory, the covenants, the giving of the law, the worship, and the promises' (*Rom.* 9:4). But what these Jewish-Christians, like Paul, had come to appreciate (according to the traditional understanding of this letter) was *not* that Gentiles could belong to this covenant too, but that they themselves, despite their privileges, were not true members simply by observing the law. They, too, like these Gentiles, had come to see that *justification* is by faith (faith in Jesus Christ) and *not* by the works of the law.

Since verse 16 forms a pivotal point in this letter, and furthermore has received a great deal of attention in recent decades, it will be helpful for us to take a more detailed look at what Paul is saying. Three phrases need our attention:

1. 'works of the law',
2. 'justified by faith',
3. 'through faith in Jesus Christ'.

## GALATIANS 2:16

'We know that a person is not justified by works of the law but through faith in Jesus Christ, so we also have believed in Christ Jesus, in order to be justified by faith in Christ and not by works of the law, because by works of the law no one will be justified' (2:16). What does Paul mean by the 'works of the law' in this verse? It is the first of six references in Galatians chapters 2 and 3. The phrase also occurs twice (three times in the KJV) in Romans as well as the singular 'the work of the law' (*Rom.* 3:20, 28). Since it occurs here in verse 16 in close proximity to the phrase 'justified by faith,' the meaning of the one cannot be considered in isolation from the other.

There are two conflicting views of these words:

i. 'Works of the law' means things like circumcision and the food laws *only*. There is no doubt that these are the very issues Paul has been dealing with in his response to the 'men from James' and the response of Peter and Barnabas. It was over these very issues that they had capitulated and refused to have table-fellowship with the Gentiles after initially engaging in it. It would make some sense, then, for Paul now to say that we are not justified because of these things.

In this case, it is argued, 'justified' must also be understood in a narrower sense to mean 'membership of God's church' or 'membership within the covenant community'. Paul is dealing with external membership in God's Church rather than with the way we are accepted in God's sight despite being sinners who have broken his law. Paul is saying something like this: *We are not considered members of the covenant community because we possess the badge of circumcision.* That is a fairly radical statement for Jews to hear, but is it the gist of what Paul is saying here? If this is so, recent interpretations of Paul go on to suggest, Paul is not thinking of our relationship to the works of the law in terms of *obedience* so much as *possession.*

It has become customary in the Protestant tradition to interpret Paul as saying that we cannot *earn* our way into the kingdom of God. The Protestant view of justification, formulated in opposition to medieval Catholicism, emphasizes that we are not justified by *merit* on our part, but freely by grace alone. Recent students of Paul understand him as saying something very different. He is concerned merely to indicate that Gentiles can be considered as members on the basis of their faith in Jesus Christ without any consideration of such things as circumcision or dietary issues. The problem is not one of a faulty understanding of *how* we enter the kingdom (by works of obedience or by faith). Rather, the fault lay in an understanding of who can belong to the kingdom (Gentiles as well as Jews). The Jews needed to appreciate that the gospel is also for those who are not circumcised.

Restricting Paul's understanding of the expression 'works of the law' here, as well as in Romans, *also restricts Paul's understanding of the work of Christ*, because he sees a direct correlation between the two. The 'faith' here in verse 16 which is associated with justification, is associated four verses later with Jesus Christ and his death on the cross: 'The life I now live in the flesh I live by faith in the Son of God, who loved me and gave himself for me' (2:20). According to this 'narrow' interpretation of 'the works of the law', Paul must necessarily restrict his understanding of what Christ accomplished on the cross. The main purpose of Christ's work on the cross was in order that the gospel need not be confined to the Jews! Paul is exulting in the cross because he has come to appreciate its multi-ethnic nature. This, it needs to be said, is a drastic reformulation of the Christian understanding of the atonement.

ii. The older and more consistent interpretation of the phrase here in Galatians understands it in parallel with its usage in Romans. In Romans 3:20, Paul writes, 'For by works of the law no human being will be justified in his sight, since through the law comes knowledge of sin.' This is Paul's conclusion following sixty-two verses (beginning in Romans 1:18) of exposition as to the nature of sin. Paul is emphasizing sin, and not just the error of restricting salvation to the circumcised! It is sin that bars our fellowship with God and any self-effort on our part only exacerbates the problem.

It appears then that Paul is saying that we are not justified by our obedience to the law. It is our relationship to a holy God that is in view, rather than our membership of the covenant community. How then are we justified? Paul's answer is 'through faith in Jesus Christ'. Again, recent interpretations have favoured the view that Paul is not referring to *our* faith so much as *Christ's faith*. Since we cannot obey the law, Jesus' *faithfulness* saves us. This is true enough in itself, but it is unlikely to be what Paul meant. He has Genesis 15:6 particularly in mind – the faith of Abraham through which he was justified: 'He believed the Lord, and he counted it to him as righteousness.' It is not the Lord's faithfulness, but Abraham's trust in the Lord that is in view.

## IMPUTED RIGHTEOUSNESS

Paul concludes by saying, 'By the works of the law no one will be justified.' He is citing Psalm 143:2. He will cite it again when he writes in similar vein to the Romans (*Rom.* 3:20). We are counted as righteous ('justified') not through the works of the law but through faith in Jesus Christ. It is the language, in embryo here, of the 'great exchange' whereby our sins are counted as Christ's and his righteousness counted as ours. 'For our sake he made him to be sin who knew no sin, so that in him we might become the righteousness of God' (*2 Cor.* 5:21). It will be the same conclusion that Paul will arrive at in verse 21: 'If justification were through the law, then Christ died for no purpose.'

The traditional interpretation of this verse is the correct one. Paul is arguing for a *judicial* understanding of justification in which God pardons sinners (law-violators), accepting them as just, and putting

[59]

them in a permanently right relationship with himself. He does this through the instrumentality of faith in Jesus Christ.

## OBJECTIONS ANSWERED

Paul is not finished. He now – and this is so typical of him – answers objections to his argument. More than likely they appear here in the very language that 'the men from James' had used, and to which Peter had yielded. We might paraphrase them syllogistically in the following way:

*ARGUMENT No. 1* (verse 17):

Paul, you say that our justification is due to our relationship to Jesus Christ.
But, you are sinning when you disobey the (dietary) laws.
*Therefore*, you are bringing Jesus Christ into sin.

*PAUL'S ANSWER* (verse 18):

Any view that says we are justified by our obedience is wrong (this is an unstable house, easily torn down!)
Your view is that we need to obey dietary laws in order to be justified.
*Therefore*, your view is wrong.

*ARGUMENT No. 2:*

Any view that says we don't need to obey in order to be justified will encourage lawlessness! (*Paul will discuss this objection again in Romans 6:1–2*).
You say, we don't need to obey these dietary laws.
*Therefore*, your view is wrong.

*PAUL'S ANSWER* (verse 19):

Lawlessness is encouraged only if I have no relationship to Jesus Christ.
But in abandoning self-effort for justification I am now in union with Christ.

*Therefore*, I want to live my whole life in a way that will please him (I have died to the law so that I might live for Christ).

## LIFE AFTER DEATH

This response of Paul's needs some elaboration. Four statements follow in quick succession:

1. 'I died to the law' (2:19). As we have already seen, Paul is concerned with more than just circumcision or the food-laws. Paul is arguing a general case at this point. There is a sense in which he has died to the law in its totality. This was a much more offensive statement to these 'men from James' than we could possibly imagine, for it sounded to them as a denial of everything Jewish, a renunciation of their entire heritage.

It is imperative that we recall throughout this section that Paul is dealing with justification and not sanctification. In renouncing the law, Paul is not abandoning, say, the role of the ten commandments in promoting and giving structure to a life of holiness. He is not ruling out the need for obedience to God's law. Paul is rather arguing that *as far as justification is concerned*, the law cannot save; it can only damn. I am dead to it *as a means of justification, of securing my acceptance as righteous before God*.

2. 'I have been *crucified* with Christ' (2:20; see *Rom.* 6:8–10; 8:10). It must have sounded particularly shocking for Paul to suggest that he had any part in Christ's crucifixion. It still does! Paul is not suggesting that anything he has done has *added* to what Christ accomplished in his death. Rather, he is drawing on the doctrine of our union with Christ as believers. When Christ died to the law's curse, we also died to it. In union with Christ we share in the great redemptive moments associated with Christ: we are thereby crucified, buried, raised and ascended in him (see *Rom.* 6:1–4; *Eph.* 2:6; *Col.* 2:6–3:4). Since Christ (with whom we are united) has borne the sting of the curse *for us*, we are dead to its pains. 'Engrafted into the death of Christ, we derive a secret energy from it, as the shoot does from the root' (Calvin). Freed from the law's curse (its sting of death), we are freed to live the way God intended. Paul will return to this in his closing remarks to this letter (6:14).

3. 'It is no longer I who live, but Christ who lives in me' (2:20). There is no suggestion here of the death of Paul's personality! He goes on to suggest otherwise: 'the life I now live . . .' But the 'I' is different! It is no longer the fallen, Adamic, 'I' but a new 'I'. The 'new man in Christ' is entirely different from the 'old man in Adam'. 'Therefore, if anyone is in Christ, he is a new creation. The old has passed away; behold, the new has come' (*2 Cor.* 5:17).

4. This radical change does not mean that we are released from spiritual conflicts; indeed, we are deeply involved in them. For *we do not yet enjoy the full consequences of this union — those consequences which we shall eventually enjoy in heaven, in a life free from sin.* In fact the gospel creates a startling tension in us. 'And the life I now live in the flesh I live by faith in the Son of God, who loved me and gave himself for me' (2:20). Every Christian lives in two worlds: 'in the flesh' and 'in Christ (by faith)'. If we place what Paul says here in parallel with what he says in Romans 7:17 we will get the picture more clearly:

| GALATIANS 2:20 | ROMANS 7:17–20 |
|---|---|
| *Life in Christ:* | *Life in the flesh:* |
| I have been crucified with Christ. It is no longer I who live, but *Christ who lives in me.* | So now it is no longer I who do it, but *sin that dwells within me.* |
| | For I know that nothing good dwells in me, that is in my flesh . . . |
| | Now if I do what I do not want, it is no longer I who do it, but *sin that dwells within me.* |

The anomaly of life before the consummation is that both the Spirit *and* sin dwell in the same person – at war with one another, until eventually the Spirit triumphs.

Notice two things here:

1. The way *our* faith and *God's* work are mutually related. Something has happened to the believer that can only be explained in terms of the sovereign operation of God. At the same time, it does not, indeed it *cannot*, take place apart from personal faith. This co-operation in no way calls into question the exercise of sovereignty on God's part.

2. The work of God in uniting the believer to Christ, so that 'Christ . . . lives in me' (2:20), is, in chapter 3, attributed to the Holy Spirit (3:2, 5, 14). The Spirit's work is one of uniting us to Jesus Christ. It is in Christ and in union with him alone that we find our justification, our redemption, our fulness, and our purpose for existence. We must therefore ensure that we drink at no other fountain.

We have reached the end of chapter 2. Paul is summing up. Had grace been obtainable through law-keeping (as the men from James were implying) then 'Christ died for no purpose' (2:21). It is as simple, and *as shocking*, as that. The attempt to reintroduce law-keeping *as a means of securing our justification* was a denial of the gospel itself. It was to cast a slur on the work Jesus had accomplished at Calvary. It was saying that his death was incomplete and insufficient to save us.

Some things need to be said clearly and plainly.

# 9

# Begun by the Spirit, Completed by the Flesh?

*O foolish Galatians! Who has bewitched you? It was before your eyes that Jesus Christ was publicly portrayed as crucified. ² Let me ask you only this: Did you receive the Spirit by works of the law or by hearing with faith? ³ Are you so foolish? Having begun by the Spirit, are you now being perfected by the flesh? ⁴ Did you suffer so many things in vain – if indeed it was in vain? ⁵ Does he who supplies the Spirit to you and works miracles among you do so by works of the law, or by hearing with faith – ⁶ just as Abraham 'believed God, and it was counted to him as righteousness'?*

*⁷ Know then that it is those of faith who are the sons of Abraham. ⁸ And the Scripture, foreseeing that God would justify the Gentiles by faith, preached the gospel beforehand to Abraham, saying, 'In you shall all the nations be blessed.' ⁹ So then, those who are of faith are blessed along with Abraham, the man of faith* (Gal. 3:1–9).

Paul was never one for disguising his true feelings. The Galatians are fools! Someone has cast 'an evil eye' on them (3:1). Satanic forces lie behind it. They have been duped. J. B. Phillips's translation here is, 'Surely you cannot be so idiotic?'

What has caused Paul to be so confrontational? Why the aggression in his tone? He began the letter by calling them 'brothers' (1:11), and will later call them 'my little children' (4:19). Even in this passage he suggests that their initial stand for the gospel was so clear that they had suffered persecution for it (3:4, though the word 'suffer' may have a broader sense). Why the change of tone?

Paul is not writing them off as false converts. But he is calling into question their understanding of the gospel. 'The truth of the gospel' was jeopardized by what had happened in Antioch, and the church in Galatia was now in danger (2:5, 14). Peter's conduct had illustrated the problem. He had yielded to pressure from Jerusalem (and from Galatia?) and had stopped eating at the same table as Gentile Christians. His actions (if not his words) had signalled that there was something that these Gentile 'Christians' had yet *to do* if they were to be fully accepted within the fold.

Paul had responded in the strongest possible manner. To suggest such a thing, he says, is to call into question the *gracious* character of our salvation. It is reintroducing what is endemic in fallen man: the gravitational pull towards self-justification through human effort and accomplishment. It is not just Gentiles who are being threatened but Jews too. Paul is concerned with much more than food-laws and whether or not Gentiles are fully acceptable; the very gospel itself is being threatened. Paul is implying here, and again later in chapter 5, that it is characteristic of 'life in the flesh' to cling to the shadows rather than to fulfilment in Christ.

To underline how crucial the issue is, Paul makes a direct appeal to the Galatians (3:1b), reminding them of what seems to have been three vital elements of his own preaching to them:

1. *Christ.* It was Jesus Christ that Paul had preached! Lest the issue be lost in the details of Paul's argument over law and gospel, he wants them to be reminded again that the gospel, and Christianity itself, is about a Person – Jesus Christ.

2. *Crucifixion.* Paul had preached Jesus as crucified. The tense implies something that has been completed. Nothing needs to be added to it in any way. All of the apostle's hope is based upon what Jesus accomplished at Calvary. We need to be reminded just how offensive crucifixion was to a Jew like Paul; yet it is the very thing in which he boasts (6:14)! And it was *this* that was in danger of being undermined.

3. *Clarity*. Paul says that Jesus Christ was 'publicly portrayed' as crucified before them. No one listening to the apostle's preaching in Galatia could fail to grasp what it was about. As they listened, it was as though Calvary itself had been brought before their eyes.

## RECEIVING THE SPIRIT

We have come to the very heart of the epistle, the point at which Paul unravels the crucial theological issue. And there is to be no avoiding of *theology*! Paul makes them *think*. By asking rhetorical questions, he forces them to think through their position. It is a measure of how far removed we are from the New Testament world that today we would be more likely to hear someone asking, 'And how do you *feel* about this?'

The question is, 'Did you receive the Spirit by works of the law or by hearing with faith?' (3:2). He will repeat the question again in verse 5. By saying, 'Let me ask you only this,' Paul evidently thinks the answer will make everything clear. Several things need to be noted so as to help us understand the force of his question more fully:

1. 'The works of the law.' The expression has already been used in 2:16 in relation to justification, and Paul is continuing the theme here. The principal 'works' under discussion were circumcision and the food laws, but Paul is here making a general point. The issues being discussed had signalled an error in their understanding of the relationship between the law and the way a person is brought into a saving relationship with God.

2. 'Receiving the Spirit.' Whereas we would perhaps speak of 'conversion' to signal the point at which we 'become Christians', the early church talked about 'receiving the Spirit' (*Rom.* 8:15; *1 Cor.* 2:12; *2 Cor.* 11:4). Paul will use the expression again, using Abraham as an example (3:14). It was what they had heard Peter say on the Day of Pentecost, 'Repent and be baptized every one of you in the name of Jesus Christ for the forgiveness of your sins, and you will receive the gift of the Holy Spirit' (*Acts* 2:38; see also 10:47; 19:2). Anyone who does not 'have the Spirit' is not a Christian (*Rom.* 8:9).

The New Testament can describe the same event – conversion – from two different perspectives. On the one hand, it is a receiving of the Holy Spirit (in addition to 3:2 and the other verses quoted, see *John* 7:39). On the other hand, at conversion the Spirit is given by the Father (*Luke* 11:13).

It is the Spirit himself that is received rather than something that the Spirit gives. The Spirit is the 'seal' (*Eph.* 4:30). A confusion on this point has led to divergent views of the Spirit's ministry.

3. 'Hearing with faith.' How had the Galatians first received the Spirit? The answer is that they had *heard* Paul preach the good news of Jesus' death *and they had responded by believing it*. They had come to God *by faith* following something they had *heard*. 'So faith comes from hearing, and hearing through the word of Christ' (*Rom.* 10:17). It is the fact that they had come into a right relationship with God *through faith alone and not by any obedience to the law* that is the main point here. Paul had not insisted that they engage in any ritual obedience prior to their acceptance in the community of the redeemed.

Having secured from them the answer he desired – that they had received the Spirit by responding by faith alone in the finished work of Christ on the cross – he now asks another question: 'Having begun by the Spirit, are you now being perfected [or, 'perfecting yourselves'?] by the flesh?' (3:3)?

## THE ROLE OF THE LAW IN THE CHRISTIAN LIFE
What precisely is Paul asking here?

1. Is Paul suggesting that just as the law plays no part in our initial conversion, so it plays no part in our on-going sanctification? It is sometimes argued that what Paul is advocating here is that just as we are justified *by faith*, so, equally, we are sanctified *by faith* – without resorting to the category of 'obligation' or 'ought'. This view is given some support by the translation of the NIV, which renders 'by the flesh' as 'by human effort'. Just as we begin without any requirement of obedience to law, we are to continue in the same way. One need only glance at the closing remarks of chapter 5 to see that

Paul expects the Galatian Christians *to refrain from doing* certain things and *to do* certain other things. Clearly, obedience does play a part in our sanctification and growth in grace!

2. Some argue that true spirituality has nothing to do with the body ('the flesh'). It is the spiritual that matters and not the earthly or material. This view has more affinity with Greek philosophy than robust biblical teaching. For Paul, what we do with our bodies defines the quality of our spirituality (*Rom.* 8:4, 11, 13).

3. Is Paul suggesting that faith gets us into the Christian fold, but to really advance our status ('to be perfected') we need to add something else? That we may be Christians, but to be 'real' Christians we need to conform to certain rules and regulations? That to be *fully* accepted more extreme measures are called for?

4. On the contrary. Note that the contrast here is not between 'flesh' and 'faith' but between 'flesh' and 'Spirit'. We have already noted that the New Testament uses 'receiving the Spirit' as synonymous with 'being a Christian'. One of the marks of the age of the Spirit (confirmed by the apostolic sign–gifts, or 'miracles' that the Galatians had witnessed, 3:5) was that obedience to the ceremonial law was not a requirement, since that aspect of the law had been fulfilled by Jesus Christ. To now insist that such obedience was necessary was to return to the age of the flesh. It would be like returning to live in the Old Testament where detailed prescriptions were laid out and which the believer had to obey. It would be as though Jesus Christ had not yet come into the world. It would be to deny that Jesus' death had ended the ceremonial law.

## ABRAHAM

It had been necessary for Paul to remind the Galatians of his visit to them, and the content of his preaching. Presently, they were despising both his person and his preaching. For Paul to be sure of their allegiance, he proceeded to appeal to something that none of his opponents could refute: his relationship to the father of the faith: *Abraham.*

Paul will now embark on the first of three major arguments from the Scriptures (the Old Testament!) to underline the truth of his own position (3:6–9; 3:15–25; 4:21–31). To those 'men from James' who had come from Jerusalem to Antioch, and to the Judaizing faction in Galatia (were they one and the same?), these arguments would prove far more pointed than anything Paul has said thus far. All three arguments will have Abraham as a common theme.

Hardly any text in the Old Testament was more crucial for the early church than Genesis 15:6: 'And [Abraham] believed the Lord, and he counted it to him as righteousness.' Paul also uses it to considerable effect in Romans 4:3. This passage is important for many reasons:

1. It refers to someone whom the Judaizers in Galatia (and Jerusalem) regarded as the 'father of the faithful'. No figure in Jewish history could have greater significance than Abraham. To appeal to him would gain their attention, and undermine their position at the same time.

2. The reference in Genesis occurs at a point which has deep significance *historically*. The passage in question occurs in Genesis 15, two chapters *before* the introduction of the requirement of circumcision as a sign and seal of the covenant that God made with Abraham. What is true of Abraham in this verse, is true of him *apart from any consideration of his being circumcised*.

3. Genesis 15:6 records in unmistakable terms Abraham's justification, that is, God's reckoning of him as righteous. The point is that Abraham was reckoned to be righteous not on the basis of anything he had done, or even would do, but upon his believing the promises of God made to him. It is an example of justification by faith alone in the promised Christ alone. The word 'counted' comes from the realm of wages being credited to a worker.

Just in case they have not understood the conclusion, Paul asserts in the plainest possible of terms: 'Know then that it is those of faith who are the sons of Abraham' (3:7). If we are going to claim allegiance to Abraham, we must be initiated into the family in precisely the same way that he was – by faith. And only those who have faith can be considered true sons of Abraham, regardless of whatever else they may share in common with him. Physical descent from, or genetic identity with, Abraham does not entitle us to be called 'sons of Abraham' in the spiritual sense. As Jesus himself said in no uncertain terms: it is possible to claim physical descent from Abraham and be a child of the devil (*John* 8:31-44).

What Genesis 15:6 provided was a prediction for the way of salvation for Gentiles, for those who would never receive circumcision as a religiously significant ritual. In a breathtaking statement, Paul attributes to Scripture the divine quality of foreknowledge (3:8). When Scripture speaks, God speaks. The Bible is God's Word. The promise that Abraham received, that through him all 'the families of the earth' would be blessed (*Gen.* 12:3) was a prediction of the salvation of the Gentiles as well as the Jews. Both would be received by God in the same way: through faith in God's promise of a Saviour.

Two important issues have been settled:

1. The true children of Abraham are those reckoned righteous through faith

2. Paul's own calling as 'the apostle to the Gentiles' finds its roots in God's Word to Abraham. Paul is claiming Abraham as his source (3:9).

The Judaizers have had the ground taken away from under their feet!

# 10

# *Redeemed from the Curse of the Law*

*For all who rely on works of the law are under a curse; for it is written, 'Cursed be everyone who does not abide by all things written in the Book of the Law, and do them.'* [11] *Now it is evident that no one is justified before God by the law, for 'The righteous shall live by faith.'* [12] *But the law is not of faith, rather 'The one who does them shall live by them.'* [13] *Christ redeemed us from the curse of the law by becoming a curse for us-for it is written, 'Cursed is everyone who is hanged on a tree'* - [14] *so that in Christ Jesus the blessing of Abraham might come to the Gentiles, so that we might receive the promised Spirit through faith* (Gal. 3:10–14).

Paul is in the middle of a tightly reasoned argument. He is making a fundamental point of immense significance. He has reminded the Galatians that they had 'received the Spirit' (Paul's way of referring to their conversion) by faith and not by an act (or acts) of obedience on their part.

He had even pulled the rug from under them by discussing Abraham. As Jewish Christians, they held Abraham in the highest esteem. We might say that he was their 'hero'. But by citing a verse from Genesis 15 in which the Patriarch was said to be 'counted . . . as righteous', Paul had actually demolished their insistence on law-keeping as a way to be justified. Abraham's circumcision (the specific law-keeping that was in view in Galatia) was not accomplished until Genesis 17, two chapters after he has already been described as justified.

Abraham was not justified 'by the works of the law'. Why, then, are they insisting that the Gentiles be justified 'by the works of the law' for them to be considered true sons of Abraham?

Paul is not finished with his argument. Indeed, he has barely begun! You can almost sense the tension mounting as Paul proceeds towards his most important point. In addition to the fact that not even Abraham himself was justified by the works of the law, there is another, more serious *and fatal* matter. The law condemns rather than justifies.

## THE CURSE OF THE LAW

Genesis was the source for Paul's first argument, and his second is based on several Old Testament passages, ranging from Deuteronomy to Habakkuk.

The first comes from Deuteronomy 27. Before we examine it in detail, it will be helpful to remember the context in which it is found. The events of the book of Deuteronomy occurred just *before* Israel crossed over the River Jordan into the Promised Land. They had spent forty years in the wilderness and God provided for them an extended reminder of who they were and what he had promised them.

In chapters 27 and 28, the twelve tribes are gathered together, six of them on Mount Gerizim and six on Mount Ebal. A litany of blessings for obedience is pronounced and another of curses for disobedience. The entire assembly shout 'Amen'. It is the concluding curse that Paul cites here. 'Cursed be everyone who does not abide by all things written in the Book of the Law, and do them' (3:10, citing *Deut.* 27:26). Paul would get to know these curses very well indeed! When, later, he would receive the thirty-nine lashes across his back (five times, *2 Cor.* 11:24), he would be required to hear them being read as the punishment was inflicted.

It would be understandable that someone might think that Paul's concern here is with circumcision – the issue which had caused Peter, Barnabas and the others to withdraw from uncircumcised Gentiles in Antioch, thereby calling into question their (the Gentiles') conversion. But Paul has a more general point to make. *The law can never justify!*

We need to examine this carefully, since it forms the axis on which the entire book turns.

Paul is making a point about 'the law'. Some have thought that what he had in view was something particular about the Mosaic Law, rather than law in general. The entire history of Israel had been, in effect, a portrayal of the way the curses of the Mosaic Law had been inflicted, in plagues, 'natural' disasters, famine, disease, military losses and exile. Even now, as these agitators in Galatia (and Jerusalem) were all too aware, they were subject to the occupying forces of the Roman Empire. The attempts to keep the law had brought Israel under the curse of occupation. What these Christian Jews needed to understand was that God now had a way for the Gentiles also to be a part of the kingdom – and that this way had nothing to do with obeying these rules and regulations that the Jews had held so dear as a distinctive mark of their ethnic identity.

But this is an altogether too narrow a view of what Paul is saying. When Paul goes on to say that Christ has redeemed 'us' from the law's curse (3:13) he has in mind both Jews *and* Gentiles. Gentiles, too, are under a curse, even though they did not possess the law in its Mosaic form. As Paul argues in the opening chapters of Romans, Gentiles as well as Jews are guilty before God. None is righteous!

## THE JUST SHALL LIVE BY FAITH

The second quotation comes from the prophet Habakkuk. It is to the effect that 'the righteous shall live by faith' (*Hab.* 2:4). This verse is cited three times in the New Testament (*Rom.* 1:17; *Heb.* 10:38). Paul has already, in his first argument of verses 6–9, referred to Abraham as an example of someone who was justified by faith (rather than by obedience to 'the works of the law'). Now he adds what was, no doubt, a well-known text in order to buttress further his argument from 'the other end' of the Old Testament.

His third quotation returns to the books of Moses again, this time to Leviticus 18:5. Paul wants to show the utter antithesis between a view of justification based on obedience to the law and one based on faith in Jesus Christ. It is impossible to hold both positions (though, no doubt, there may well have been some who were trying to do just that!). Leviticus 18:5 states that 'The one who does them shall live by them.' Paul's point is to show that law and faith are opposites; that 'the law is not of faith' (3:12). If you begin by insisting on obedience as the way of salvation, you are committed to a view of *complete* obedience and not partial obedience. You cannot begin with obedience and then add faith somewhere along the line. It is 'all or nothing'. It is not enough to keep this or that law; obedience, if it is to be a means of justification, must be absolute and total. James makes a similar point: 'For whoever keeps the whole law but fails in one point has become accountable for all of it' (*James* 2:10).

Leviticus 18:5 is cited in two further passages in the New Testament. In Romans 10:5, Paul – in a very similar argument to the one before us here in Galatians 3 – again shows the complete antithesis between justification by obedience to the law and justification by faith in Jesus Christ. The other occasion is found in the introduction to Jesus' parable of the Good Samaritan in Luke 10. A lawyer asked Jesus what he could *do* to inherit the kingdom of God. Jesus asked the man what the law would say to this question. The man replied by citing the 'two great commandments': love for God and for one's neighbour. Then Jesus said (citing Leviticus 18:5), 'Do this, and you will live' (*Luke* 10:28).

But we are now faced with a dilemma. If obedience to the law is not possible, if the curse is inevitable for both Jew and Gentile, how can anyone be saved? The letter to the Galatians was written to answer this very question!

## THE PROMISE OF ABRAHAM

The way of justification by obedience to the law has proved a futile journey. It has brought only a curse. And the agitators in Galatia and Jerusalem will only bring further condemnation upon themselves if they now insist that obedience is a necessary prerequisite for the Gentiles to be fully accepted into the Christian fold. The law will always show us up as sinners! How is it possible then for anyone to be saved? The answer, of course, is by faith in Jesus Christ who has perfectly obeyed the law in its totality for us!

In many ways, Leviticus 18:5, with its insistence on obedience to the law, has pointed the way to Jesus Christ. It anticipated all along that he would be the only one able to perform its demands. And lest we miss the point, Paul puts it in the clearest possible terms:

'Christ redeemed us from the curse of the law by becoming a curse for us' (3:13). Although it is the law that 'curses' in this passage, it is God the Father who issues this curse – the law is but a reflection of his holy nature. Indeed, in the passage from which Paul now quotes – Deuteronomy 21:23 – it is specifically *God's* curse that is mentioned. Jesus, God's Son, was smitten by God and afflicted (*Isa.* 53:4–6; *Matt.* 27:46).

The curse inflicted upon the Son ('curse' here means 'the cursed one') was that he would know the Father's unmitigated wrath poured out upon him. Behind this verse lies the darkness of the cry of dereliction from the cross, 'My God, my God, why have you forsaken me?' (*Matt.* 27:46; *Mark* 15:34). The price of redemption was the alienation of the Son from the Father. In the language of the Apostles' Creed, 'He descended into hell.'

It is tempting to think (as some have argued) that this verse was already known to the early Christians and is here quoted as an axiom of Christian theology. One can hardly imagine anything more basic for a Christian to know than that which this verse insists upon. In it we are introduced to a key Bible-word, *'redemption'*.

Jews as well as Gentiles would know this word well. They would be familiar with it from the *agora*, or market-place. It was the everyday word in commerce for purchase. In particular, it would have been familiar to them from the language of purchasing and selling slaves. Christians enslaved to sin are 'purchased' by the blood of Christ. The price of their redemption is the death of Jesus Christ. And his death is a *cursed* death. It is something inflicted upon him, taken up by him, rather than something 'natural.' The curse of a broken covenant was laid upon him. Jesus died the death of a transgressor.

The *form* of his death – death by crucifixion – highlights the cursed nature of it. Paul cites Deuteronomy 21:23 to underline that 'hanging on a tree' was considered a cursed death.

In addition to the biblical idea of redemption, two more concepts are needed to understand what Paul is saying here. They are the concepts of *penal substitution* and *satisfaction*.

1. *Substitution.* Since Jesus was sinless, the cursed nature of his death must be accounted for in terms other than a punishment for his own sin. He died *for* us (3:13). The preposition 'for' is crucial. It occurs again in a similar passage in 2 Corinthians: 'For (*huper*) our sake he made him to be sin who knew no sin, so that in him we might become the righteousness of God' (*2 Cor.* 5:21). Martin Luther's advice to a young Christian troubled with assurance still rings true:

> Learn Christ and him crucified. Learn to pray to him and, despairing of yourself, say: 'Thou Lord Jesus, art my righteousness, but I am thy sin. Thou hast taken upon thyself what is mine and hast given to me what is thine. Thou hast taken upon thyself what thou wast not and hast given to me what I was not.'

2. *Satisfaction.* The death of Jesus was not only substitutionary; it was also a perfect fulfilment of what the law (God!) required. He offered a perfect obedience in our place. He satisfied the demands of the law in all its details.

## CONCLUSION

Paul has reached a point of conclusion. Faith in Jesus Christ (rather than obedience to the law) brings three things:

1. *Justification.* The blessing of Abraham which he had referred to earlier in the first half of this chapter.

2. *Inclusion.* That Gentiles as well as Jews might be received into the kingdom in exactly the same way. Christ has redeemed us by becoming a curse for us (Jews as well as Gentiles) that we (Jews as well as Gentiles) might receive the promised Holy Spirit. There is nothing about the Jew now that distinguishes him from Gentiles as far as the way of salvation is concerned.

3. *The Gift of the Spirit.* Faith brings the promise of the Spirit (in the objective sense: the promised Spirit). Christ lives in us (2:20) by means of the Holy Spirit who is the Spirit of God's Son (4:6). The

giving of the Spirit is the fulfilment of the promise of the New Covenant. It is interesting to note in this regard that it was precisely the *poured out* Spirit to whom Peter drew attention on the day of Pentecost. Peter, in fact, referred to two related issues: the request of Jesus and the pouring out of the Spirit. In Acts 2:33 Peter draws attention to the fact that the ascended Christ pleads the promise of Psalm 2:6–8:

> I have set my King on Zion, my holy hill.
> I will tell of the decree:
> The Lord said to me, 'You are my Son;
> > today I have begotten you.
> Ask of me, and I will make the nations your heritage,
> > and the ends of the earth your possession.'

Following the ascension, victory having been gained, Christ asked for the Spirit to be poured out ( *Joel* 2:28–30). As evidence of Christ's enthronement, the Spirit is poured out on all flesh. In particular, he is poured out upon the Gentiles, in fulfilment of the ancient promise to Abraham (*Gen.* 12:3). Christ underwent the covenant curse so that the blessing given to Abraham might be fulfilled in the gift of the Holy Spirit to all those who believe, whether Jew or Gentile.

It might be helpful at this point to remind ourselves that the Lord's Supper is a remembrance of this cursed death. In his death he has borne the judgment curse for us in order that he might share with us the blessings of the presence of God.

# Law and Promise

*To give a human example, brothers: even with a man-made
covenant, no one annuls it or adds to it once it has been ratified.
[16] Now the promises were made to Abraham and to his offspring.
It does not say, 'And to offsprings,' referring to many, but
referring to one, 'And to your offspring,' who is Christ. [17] This is
what I mean: the law, which came 430 years afterward, does
not annul a covenant previously ratified by God, so as to make
the promise void. [18] For if the inheritance comes by the law, it no
longer comes by promise; but God gave it to Abraham by a
promise (Gal. 3:15–18).*

In the first part of Paul's argument he has cited the Scriptures six
times (3:6–14). He has argued that Jesus Christ's death on the
cross has purchased salvation for both Jews and Gentiles. In so doing,
Jesus has fulfilled a promise that had been given to Abraham at the
beginning. Gentiles, as well as Jews, become full members of the
kingdom of God by faith in the finished work of Jesus Christ, *not* by
obedience to the law.

A potential problem now arises. In setting the way of justification
*against* the law, Paul was in danger of pitting Moses *against* Christ.
In alluding to Abraham (five times in the previous section, 3:6–14,
and twice more in this section, 3:16,18), Paul is in further danger of
pitting Moses *against* Abraham. This needs some explanation lest
Paul be misunderstood, and the relationship between the Old and
New Testaments be set in irremediable jeopardy. In providing such
an explanation, Paul resorts to using several important words. They

are *covenant, promise* and *inheritance*. In order to understand what Paul regards as foundational – the gospel itself – we will need to appreciate the meaning of these words!

## AN UNBREAKABLE COVENANT

Having mentioned in verse 14 that the Gentiles receive the Spirit (become Christians) in the same way as Jews, Paul has introduced the (as yet unstated) idea that Christian Jews and Christian Gentiles belong to the same family. And because of this, it is unhelpful for us to go on referring to them as Christian *Jews* and Christian *Gentiles*. There are no distinctions any more in the kingdom of God between Jews and Gentiles.

Paul will put it emphatically at the close of this chapter: 'There is neither Jew nor Greek, there is neither slave nor free, there is neither male nor female, for you are all one in Christ Jesus' (3:28). As though he were underlining this thought, Paul addresses the Galatians as 'brothers' (3:15), something which he has not done since the first chapter (1:11).

Few things have vexed the church more, particularly those of us who live on this side of the book of Malachi, than the relationship between Moses (and the law given at Sinai) and the rest of the Bible. If, as Paul has argued, Abraham was justified by believing the promise of the covenant that God made with him, what are we to make of the covenant made with Moses? Was this an entirely different sort of covenant, one perhaps based on 'works of obedience' rather than faith? Did God, in the period of Moses and the law, set aside what he had established with Abraham? And if so, was the law permanent or temporary? Even the best theologians have trembled here. It might be advantageous for us to anticipate what Paul says on this point *before* we examine it in detail. He puts forward two arguments:

1. A covenant, once it has been made by God, cannot be broken or annulled. Having established the way of faith and grace with Abraham, this promise cannot be taken away in the very next book of the Bible, Exodus, with its allusions to Moses and Sinai. That would make everything we know about God questionable and

uncertain. That interpretation is simply not an option. This is what Paul will say in verses 15 and 16.

2. Whatever precise function the law (given at Sinai) has, it cannot annul what God had laid down already with Abraham. Coming as it did four centuries *after* Abraham, the law at Sinai must have a subservient function. This is what Paul says in verses 17 and 18.

The Old Testament passages to which Paul refers would, of course, have been familiar to the *Jewish* Christians in Galatia. Familiarity is one thing; comprehension is another. The Galatians had heard these passages *interpreted* in a different way and the apostle must now teach them *how to read their Bibles correctly*.

Paul begins by referring, not to the Bible, but to something his readers knew to be true in everyday life. Covenants (agreements which have standing in law) cannot be changed once they are made (3:15). It is not clear whether Paul is thinking of the world of Roman, Greek, or Jewish, legal institutions. In both the Greek and Roman world it was possible to change the terms of an agreement when circumstances changed. It is certain that no one apart from the one who made the agreement could change it. Its benefactors were not at liberty to tinker with it. In that case, Paul is making a point that could easily be understood: once made, the terms of a covenant are inviolable. And what were those terms in this case? That Abraham and his posterity would be justified by faith.

Several issues that now arise require comment:

1. The original promise made to Abraham included the promise of land (*Gen.*12:1-2). However, God had also said to Abraham that *all the families of the earth* would *be blessed* in him. It is evident that something more than just the land of Canaan was in view. Whatever temporal aspects were attached to the Abrahamic covenant, as far as Paul was concerned, its essence lay in the giving of the Spirit at Pentecost, in the coming to faith in Jesus Christ of the Gentiles, and of redemption from the curse of sin. When Paul saw Gentiles coming into the kingdom in great numbers, he said, 'This is what God promised to Abraham!' It was, in fact, what Jesus meant when he gave 'the Great Commission'. To 'make disciples of all nations' was

an echo of such promises as Genesis 12:3 and 22:18 given to Abraham. The New Testament church has its roots in Genesis and in the covenant with Abraham.

2. Having used the plural, 'promises' at verse 16 (and again at verse 21), Paul then switches to the singular in half a dozen further instances in this chapter (3:17, 18 [twice], 19, 22, 29), as he had when he had first introduced the word in verse 14. Since Paul will make a great deal of the difference between 'offspring (or, *seed*)' and 'offsprings (*seeds*)' in verse 16, we must ask if the difference is significant with respect to promise and promises? Paul may well be switching in his mind from the plural (promises) as it referred to such things as land and descendants (see *Gen.* 17:7–8), to the singular (promise) when he has in mind how that promise finds fulfilment – *in the giving of the Holy Spirit.*

3. The promises were to Abraham and his descendants (*seed*). In what looks like a piece of theological hair-splitting at its worst, Paul now engages in some very precise argumentation based on the *singular* reference to 'seed', rather than the plural ('seeds'):

'for all the land that you see I will give to you and to your offspring (singular '*seed*') forever' (*Gen.* 13:15; contrast 13:16; 24:7).

The point is that Paul wants us to appreciate that the promise had reference to a singular seed, 'which is Christ' (3:16). This essentially Christian understanding and interpretation of Genesis (and of the Old Testament) has enormous ramifications. The original offspring of Abraham was Isaac, and it would have been natural for this text to be seen to refer to him. Paul, however, from the vantage point of the New Testament can see layers of meaning that Old Testament interpreters might not have seen: that implicit within this promise was a prediction of the coming of Jesus Christ.

4. The descendants (which, of course, now included Gentiles) are considered as singular, because (and this was something very dear to Paul's heart) believers are in union with Jesus Christ.

5. Paul uses a word here in verse 15 (and again in verse 17) which is translated 'covenant' even though it looks as though what is in view is a 'testament' or 'last will'. When the Jews translated their Bible into Greek, they faced the problem of how to express the Hebrew word for 'covenant': *berith*. One possibility was *syntheke*, which expressed the idea of mutuality, a compact or treaty. This word preserved one aspect of the Hebrew covenant, an agreement, but did not do justice to the predominant emphasis on God's initiative, so the translators chose *diatheke*, a word meaning 'disposition' or 'arrangement'. It is the word employed here. God's covenant with Abraham and its repeated promises (*Gen.* 12:2–3,7; 13:15; 17:7–8; 22:16–18; 24:7) is not superseded by the law, which came much later, in the time of Moses. The inheritance (of the Spirit and the blessings) is by promise, not by law (*Gal.* 3:18). Paul's argument hinges on the fact that the same Greek word, *diatheke*, can be rendered as will or testament (*Gal.* 3:15) and as covenant (*Gal.* 3:17).

## PROMISE RATHER THAN LAW

There follows a conclusion: '*for* if the inheritance comes by the law, it no longer comes by promise; but God gave it to Abraham by a promise' (3:18). Having established that within the promise made to Abraham was,

   i.   the inclusion of Gentile believers,
   ii.  the promise of the Holy Spirit,
   iii. the promise of Jesus Christ in whom all believers are united,

Paul is now ready to return to his original argument: that salvation is by faith alone in the finished work of Christ alone and not by obedience to the law. Christian (believing) Gentiles *inherit* just as do Christian (believing) Jews. They have all the legal rights of inheritance that belong to the children of Abraham.

This last point must have been shocking to the Jews of Paul's day, even to Christian Jews who had been raised to regard Gentiles as 'dogs' unworthy of common respect, let alone as fellow citizens of the kingdom of God – and *heirs*!

And if you are Christ's, then you are Abraham's offspring, heirs according to promise (3:29).

This mystery is that the Gentiles are fellow heirs, members of the same body, and partakers of the promise in Christ Jesus through the gospel (*Eph.* 3:6).

Many of the statements made by the apostle here with respect to the law are deeply troubling. If we do not find them so, we have probably not understood their import. Following Paul's arrest in the temple precincts recorded in Acts 21, the charge levelled against him was that he taught 'everyone everywhere against the people and the law and this place' (*Acts* 21:28). It may be hard for us to appreciate that Paul was being charged with *antinomianism* (with being anti-*law*), since the prevailing interpretation of the apostle's teaching is so opposite to this. But consider the following verses:

For through the law I died to the law, so that I might live to God. I have been crucified with Christ (*Gal.* 2:19).

For we hold that one is justified by faith apart from works of the law (*Rom.* 3:28).

Likewise, my brothers, you also have died to the law through the body of Christ, so that you may belong to another, to him who has been raised from the dead, in order that we may bear fruit for God . . . But now we are released from the law, having died to that which held us captive, so that we serve not under the old written code but in the new life of the Spirit (*Rom.* 7:4, 6).

It is not difficult, after reading such statements, to see why many Christians have concluded that the New Testament economy is one in which law has been abrogated in favour of grace. But one need only turn to the closing sections of this epistle and note how Paul insists on the obedience that is characteristic of the new life in Christ, to see that the function law plays is far more complex than that. We shall see later the part that the law plays in sanctification. As far as justification is concerned, it functions only negatively, as a tool that indicates our utter inability to save ourselves. It is (anticipating Paul's later comment) a schoolmaster (or *guardian*) that disciplines us away from self-reliance and, instead, towards wholehearted trust in Jesus Christ (3:24).

## 12

## *The Purpose of the Law*

*Why then the law? It was added because of transgressions, until the offspring should come to whom the promise had been made, and it was put in place through angels by an intermediary. [20] Now an intermediary implies more than one, but God is one.*

*[21] Is the law then contrary to the promises of God? Certainly not! For if a law had been given that could give life, then righteousness would indeed be by the law. [22] But the Scripture imprisoned everything under sin, so that the promise by faith in Jesus Christ might be given to those who believe. [23] Now before faith came, we were held captive under the law, imprisoned until the coming faith would be revealed. [24] So then, the law was our guardian until Christ came, in order that we might be justified by faith* (Gal 3:19–24).

On several occasions, Paul sounds as though he might be saying that he has no time for the law whatsoever. It would be easy to suggest that this is what Paul thinks! He has chastised the Galatians for yielding to the pressure of the agitators who were insisting that the Gentiles be circumcised. To this Paul has responded by saying that any attempt to look to the law for our justification (reliance on 'works of the law') is doomed to failure (3:10).

It is precisely because the law has cursed us that Christ has become 'a curse for us'. Paul understands Christ's crucifixion as the retribution of the law (3:13). As our substitute, Christ bore in himself the *penalty* of our unrighteousness in order that he might present to us (reckon to our account) his perfect righteousness. In all this, the law has served as a 'ministry of death' (*2 Cor.* 3:7). As Paul would write elsewhere, he had himself found the law to 'promise life' and yet prove to be 'death' to him (*Rom.* 7:10). Perhaps you are already anticipating the question that the apostle now asks: 'Why then the law' (3:19).

In part, the apostle has already answered the question. The law has a function in pointing out our sins. But before we examine that particular answer (the one he gives in verse 19), it might be helpful at this stage to note something of the multifaceted function of the law.

## WHY THE LAW?

The law is *God*'s law (*Rom.* 7:22, 25; 8:7; *1 Cor.* 7:19). As such, it is 'spiritual' (*Rom.* 7:14), 'holy,' 'righteous' and 'good' (*Rom.* 7:12). We must not allow this positive aspect to be overshadowed and forgotten. If the law can play no part in our justification other than to condemn, that does not mean that it has no other function to play in other aspects of our life and standing before God. The fact is that holiness is unattainable apart from obedience to the law of God. It is vital that we keep this in mind as we explore what Paul has to say here in terms of the law's relationship to us in justification. Whatever negative aspects Paul will now stress (and stress with unparalleled force he will!) they cannot be interpreted to imply a *contradiction* of what God had already promised to Abraham. The giving of the law at Sinai was not God changing his mind. *Certainly not* (3:21)!

Paul's answer to the question, 'Why then the law?' is not as simple as we might expect. It *begins* simply enough – 'it was added because of our transgressions' – but it then assumes a complexity that reminds us of Peter's comment to the effect that there are some things in Paul that are hard to understand (*2 Pet.* 3:16)! Before we delve into the deep waters of Paul's answer, it will be helpful to explore that part of the answer that appears clear-cut: the law was added because of our transgressions (3:19).

1. Paul is speaking *historically* at this point. The law was given 430 years after Abraham (3:17). Paul has already in the previous section (3:15–18) made the point that by coming *after* the covenant made with Abraham it could not in any way annul or even alter the

terms of that covenant. The function of the law (given at Sinai) was to further the terms of the covenant already made with Abraham. In some way or other, the law promotes the way of redemption as spelled out to Abraham.

2. What the law does at Sinai is show sin *as sin*: 'Now the law came in (in order) to increase the trespass, but where sin increased, grace abounded all the more' (*Rom.* 5:20). The purpose of the law was to expose the sinful condition of mankind. It 'came in by a side road', would accurately convey what Paul means. The main road is the Abrahamic covenant. What better way to show up the dirt (that already existed *before* Sinai, 'for sin indeed was in the world before the law was given, but sin is not counted where there is no law' (*Rom.* 5:13)) than to shine the light of God's law upon it?

3. The law does more than show up sin; *it makes us sin more*! Without the law, sin may lie hidden (*Rom.* 7:8). It has nothing to expose it. But the very presence of law for fallen men and women becomes the occasion for more sin. As Paul found in his own experience, 'I was once alive apart from the law, but when the commandment came, sin came alive and I died' (*Rom.* 7:9).

4. The law pronounces God's condemnation and curse. From one perspective at least, Sinai represented for Paul 'the ministry of condemnation' (*2 Cor.* 3:9). It is a point which he has been at pains to underline for the past dozen or so verses: 'For all who rely on works of the law are under a curse; for it is written, "Cursed be everyone who does not abide by all things written in the Book of the Law, and do them"' (*Gal.* 3:10; see also 3:13).

5. The law finds its fulfilment in Jesus Christ. This is what Paul eventually will say in this passage. The law shows up our sinfulness, but it does so in order to lead us to the only way of salvation: faith in Jesus Christ (3:22). Paul puts it more succinctly in Romans: 'For Christ is the end (that is, *goal*) of the law for righteousness to everyone who believes' (*Rom.* 10:4). The giving of the law served the purpose of fulfilling the promise that had been made in the covenant with Abraham – the promise of Jesus Christ!

[87]

This is, in fact, what Paul means by the statement in verse 19, 'until the offspring should come to whom the promise had been made.' If we render 'offspring' as 'Seed' (capital 'S') we immediately get the point. The law served as a pointer to the coming of Christ. It should also be noted that Paul may well have in mind another issue directly relevant to the problem at Galatia, Antioch and Jerusalem: that the kingdom of God is singular; Jews *and* Gentiles are to be considered as *one*: one in Christ! The goal of the Abrahamic covenant had been to produce a single family, 'the people of God' united together by faith in Jesus Christ. 'For he himself is our peace, who has made us both one and has broken down in his flesh the dividing wall of hostility' (*Eph.* 2:14). It is this very point that Paul will make at verse 28.

The law, then, was our guardian to lead us to Christ (3:24). The word Paul uses has given rise to a theological term – the *pedagogic* use of the law. It is meant to define that aspect of the law that initially condemns and shuts us up with no alternative but to trust in Jesus Christ for our salvation. And this, not only in our own individual experience of the law, but in the historical sense: Paul is thinking of the way the entire Old Testament period was, in a sense, a preparation (a school) for the New (graduation).

All of this is meant to demonstrate the function of the giving of the law at Sinai. It is not meant to exhaust its function, nor suggest that from now on the Christians in Galatia are not obliged to keep the law in any way or form. It has served to demonstrate one function of the law, what the Reformation termed the *pedagogic* function: to bring sinners to an end of themselves that they might embrace Jesus Christ alone. The Reformation (particularly through the insights of John Calvin in Geneva) emphasized two further uses of the law: as a rule for the ordering of society (the *civil* use), and as a rule for Christians (*already justified by faith in Jesus Christ*) to grow in holiness (the so-called *third* use of the law).

## ANGELS FROM THE REALMS OF GLORY

The main drift of what Paul is saying in these verses is clear enough. However in the course of his argument he makes several statements that are difficult to interpret.

What does Paul mean about the law being 'put in place through angels by an intermediary'? The 'intermediary' here is Moses. (Some take the reference to be to Christ, but this fits poorly in the context.) Exodus 19 makes no mention of angels at all (though the New Testament insists on it in several places, *Acts* 7:38, 53; *Heb.* 2:2). Why then does Paul mention them?

Partly, because it was common in Paul's day to interpret 'chariots of fire' in Psalm 68:17 (a reference to Sinai) as referring to angels (see also Deuteronomy 33:2); and partly, also, because angels are present at all the significant moments of redemptive history: creation (Genesis is silent, but Job 38:7 mentions their exclamations of joy at creation), the stories of the Patriarchs (*Gen.* 19:1–11; 21:17; 24:7, 40), the prophets (*1 Kings* 13:18; 19:5, 7; *2 Kings* 1:3, 15), the birth, life and death of Christ (*Luke* 1:19, 26; 2:9, 13; *Matt.* 4:11; *Luke* 22:43), the resurrection (*John* 20:12), the second coming (*Matt.* 16:27; 25:31).

It is not difficult to imagine that the period of Israel's exodus was also accompanied by the ministry of angels. The angels' fascination with the entire process of redemption could hardly keep them in heaven at such moments (*1 Pet.* 1:12)!

But Paul still has to tell us the reason why he has raised the issue of angels and a mediator (Moses). The answer lies in appreciating that an intermediary implies 'more than one, but God is one' (3:20). What can this possibly mean?

Paul wants to demonstrate that the Mosaic Covenant with its emphasis on law is subservient to the covenant established with Abraham. God had spoken singularly and directly to Abraham, whereas at Sinai God had given the law through intermediaries. The law as given at Sinai furthered the differences between Jews and Gentiles. But God's purpose as signified to Abraham was to produce one people, since he himself is one, as the ancient *Shema*, 'Hear, O Israel: The LORD our God, the LORD is one' (*Deut.* 6:4), had constantly reminded his people. Whatever function the law had at Sinai could only serve to accentuate the differences. The priority must be Abraham and not Moses.

Paul, in verse 22, indicates that the law as given at Sinai had confined or imprisoned people in order to draw them in the direction of faith in Jesus Christ as the only way of salvation. Verse 23 now continues this theme, outlining again what happened 'when faith came'.

One of the issues that have to be considered in some of Paul's writings is whether to interpret his statements in the context of the appearing of Christ on the stage of history in the first century (the history of redemption), or in the context of our *experience* of appropriating Christ.

When he says, 'Now before faith came, we were held captive under the law', is he speaking *personally* of his own Christian experience (as a pattern for all who come to faith in Christ)? Or is he describing the transition from the Old Covenant to the New – an experience of bondage (imprisonment) followed by one of liberty – and the fact that this is also the *experience* of some (or many) is beside the point? Is Paul suggesting that this is typical of the experience of every Christian? That it has been so understood has led to problems. Some Christians are awakened gently, as a mother awakens her child from sleep – with a kiss! Not all Christian conversions are alike. Some are dramatic and others are not.

It is best to understand Paul here as speaking from the point of view of *the history of redemption*. He is speaking of the change that has been effected by the coming of Christ, in the transformation from Old Testament to New Testament. He is not, of course, asserting that the way of faith was unknown *before* Christ came. The way of faith was known by Abraham. But the years from Moses to Malachi had only shown the futility of trying to be justified by the law.

Paul mentions the role of the 'pedagogue' in order to make his point ('*guardian*', 3:24, 25). It is all too easy to caricature the negative aspect of these guardians, as known in the ancient world. They were not always rude and spiteful as they are sometimes portrayed. Perhaps it will help us to understand this passage if we say a little more on the role of a *guardian*.

Generally speaking, they were slaves, taken captive during a war, and sold to well-to-do heads of households who were eager to acquire their aid in the moral upbringing of the master's children (especially his male heirs). They were *not*, as a rule, teachers. They were, rather, disciplinarians, and usually older men, perhaps of an age when strenuous physical activity was no longer possible.

A child would come under the supervision of a pedagogue at about the age of six and would continue so until the late teens. The relationship was not always severe. Indeed, there are known instances when a child bonded with his pedagogue in a remarkable way. Alexander the Great, according to Plutarch, risked his life in order to stay with his aged pedagogue Lysimachus. This was unusual, however, and more often than not the discipline inflicted by pedagogues was harsh and cruel.

What particular aspect of the pedagogue's role does Paul have in mind here when he likens the role of the law (in the Old Testament economy) to a *pedagogue*? It seems beyond doubt that Paul has something negative rather than positive in mind. It was not the function of a pedagogue to pour out affection, but to chastise and rebuke. If sons grew up to be ill-mannered and disrespectful, it was the pedagogue that was blamed! *The law, just like a pedagogue, is always pointing out our failures!*

In contrast to the period of the old covenant, there is something liberating for those who belong to the new covenant! Paul will elaborate upon this in the next section. Notice also that whilst this *historical* interpretation of verses 23–24 is the correct understanding, these verses are also exactly descriptive of the common experience of many individual Christians. The law has convicted of sin, exacerbated the sense of bondage and driven them to Christ. We need to be careful, however, not to apply this so as to suggest that every Christian must *experience* this in the same discernible or measurable way. We shall return to this point again in the next chapter.

## IMPRISONMENT

We have mentioned another term that Paul uses to help us gain an accurate understanding of the role that the law plays before the coming of Christ. It 'holds us captive.' It 'imprisons' (3:23)! No image could more graphically portray the law's function than this one. Paul envisions the Jews (especially at the time of their reception of the law at Sinai) as prisoners! The very ones now calling upon Gentile Christians to obey the law *in order to prove their justification* were in fact demanding that they join them in prison!

Paul has demonstrated that the Scriptures at this point 'imprison' us all (3:22, 24). The law shows up our sinfulness and exacerbates our fallen condition, to such an extent that the only way left open to us in which we can be saved is to exercise faith in God's Son. The question is, have we come to appreciate that fact?

# 13

## If Christ's, Then Heirs

*But now that faith has come, we are no longer under a guardian,*
*²⁶ for in Christ Jesus you are all sons of God, through faith.*
*²⁷ For as many of you as were baptized into Christ have put on*
*Christ. ²⁸ There is neither Jew nor Greek, there is neither slave*
*nor free, there is neither male nor female, for you are all one in*
*Christ Jesus. ²⁹ And if you are Christ's, then you are Abraham's*
*offspring, heirs according to promise* (Gal. 3:25–29).

If ever we were in doubt as to the authorship of a letter attributed to Paul, one of the ways we could identify it as Pauline would be to look for one of his tell-tale signs: the use of the phrase 'in Christ'. He uses it more than one hundred and sixty times in the New Testament! For the apostle, the central ministry of the Holy Spirit is to unite us to Jesus Christ and thereby unite every Christian ( Jew and Gentile) to each other in the one body. Receiving the Spirit (3:2, 5, 14) brings us into union with Christ. To become a Christian is to 'put on Christ' (3:27). And being in union with Jesus Christ implies that all the blessings of salvation are ours irrespective of *who* or *what* we were beforehand (*Eph.* 1:13–23). In Christ we are heirs of the promise of salvation. It is this that is now worked out in detail in the concluding section of chapter 3.

## THE FAMILY OF GOD
Paul now introduces an important concept, one that so far he has not mentioned: that as believers we are *the children of God*. As we saw at the close of the previous section, Paul has been unfolding the historical consequences of the coming of Christ. He has been

contrasting spiritual experience before and after Christ's coming. Is there a difference? Think of what Jesus said of John the Baptist, 'the one who is least in the kingdom of heaven is greater than he' (*Matt.* 11:11). For Paul, it was like the difference between being a child, with all the restrictions that that can often entail, and being given the keys to the car and one's own apartment! It has to do with growing up and becoming an adult.

There is, as we have insisted several times, a basic unity between the Old and New Testaments. There is *one* way of salvation, *one* faith, operating throughout the Bible. This, after all, has been Paul's point in raising the figure of Abraham earlier in the chapter (3:6-9). But there is also a dramatic change – a *development* – that takes place on stepping from the Old Testament into the pages of the New Testament. Having used two vivid metaphors to show the role of law as far as its ability to justify is concerned, a *prison* and a *pedagogue*, Paul now introduces a contrasting metaphor with breathtaking implications. New Testament believers have left the 'prison' for the 'family estate'. They have left the discipline of the pedagogue for the embrace of a welcoming Father!

In many ways this idea is central to Paul's understanding of what God is doing in the world. As he thinks about the story of redemption, Paul brings us back to this again and again: 'For those whom he foreknew he also predestined to be conformed to the image of his Son, in order that he might be the firstborn among many brothers' (*Rom.* 8:29). God's purpose is to produce a family in which Jesus Christ is the Elder Brother! He means to bring many *sons* to glory (*Heb.* 2:10). It is what Jesus' coming has been all about:

> But when the fullness of time had come, God sent forth his Son, born of woman, born under the law, to redeem those who were under the law, so that we might receive adoption as sons. And because you are sons, God has sent the Spirit of his Son into our hearts, crying, 'Abba! Father!' So you are no longer a slave, but a son, and if a son, then an heir through God. (4:4–7).

Paul's aim is not only to bring to the surface the glories of adoption; it is to make the point that the Gentiles are also considered as full members of this family. Nothing needs to be added to their faith in Jesus Christ to make them more acceptable as members of the family of God than they already are. *Nothing!* Not circumcision. Not obedience to food laws. Nothing!

## BAPTISM

Having introduced the concept of adoption, Paul now quickly introduces us to another – *baptism* (3:27). Before becoming entangled in the issues relating to *physical* baptism, we need to bear in mind that Paul is making what is first and foremost a *theological* point. What is that point? That coming to faith in Christ, receiving the Spirit, being baptized into Christ, all belong together.

Given the fact that Paul has been (and still is) dealing with the implications of the covenant with Abraham and how it relates to the economy of Moses and the law, it stands to reason that the ideas of covenant are still operative as he raises the issue of baptism. Christ underwent the covenant curse so that the blessing given to Abraham might be fulfilled in the gift of the Spirit to those who believe – Jews as well as Gentiles. That curse which Jesus bore was a *baptism* (*Luke* 12:50). New covenant believers are baptized 'into Christ' identifying with his baptism-ordeal on the cross. He was baptized with the curse of the covenant; we are baptized with the blessing of the covenant – the Holy Spirit. The Spirit's constant ministry is to draw our eyes to what Christ has done: 'He will glorify me, for he will take what is mine and declare it to you' (*John* 16:14).

Baptism, theologically considered, represents the language of union and participation. When Paul wished to convey the willingness of the Israelites to identify with Moses as their leader before the opened Red Sea, he used the language of baptism: 'And all were baptized into Moses in the cloud and in the sea' (*1 Cor.* 10:2). It is not the mode of baptism that is primarily in view – they crossed on dry land after all! The point is their *identification* with Moses and his headship over them. Similarly, believers identify with Jesus' Lordship in the baptism of the Spirit. The language of baptism is therefore expressive of our union with Christ by faith. What is ours becomes his; what is his becomes ours.

Does this mean that what Paul says here has nothing at all to do with physical baptism? Is the apostle's concern here merely spiritual?

Of course not! Paul's audience in Galatia had no doubt received water baptism and it would have been impossible then, just as it is now, for baptism to be mentioned without the thought (indeed, for those baptized as adult believers, the memory) of water baptism. Of course, Paul is not identifying water baptism as the means by which our faith union is achieved. That would contradict everything for which he has been arguing in this letter. He would not protest against the necessity of circumcision for salvation on the one hand whilst insisting on the necessity of water baptism on the other!

Water baptism functioned then, as now, as a visible sign of what Christ offers through faith. It symbolizes the removal of sin from us and the placing of it upon Christ. In that regard, it is interesting to note that the two occasions in the New Testament where an Old Testament event is called a baptism (the crossing of the Red Sea in 1 Corinthians 10:2 and the Noahic Flood in 1 Peter 3:18–21) are both occasions where blessing is brought to one party at the expense of a curse on another. Water baptism is a sign, not only of forgiveness of sins through faith in Christ, but also of the judgment ordeal that Christ suffered in order to procure for us the blessings we enjoy in union with him.

Water baptism is not only a sign; it is also a seal. It conveys to us in visible form (a *visible word*, as Augustine called it) the promise that attaches to the sign. It says in unmistakable terms that there is forgiveness for whoever believes in Jesus Christ.

## PUTTING ON CHRIST

Thus believers have 'put on Christ' (3:27). They wear Christ as they would a garment. 'They are united to Christ in such a way', writes Calvin, 'that, in the sight of God, they bear the name and person of Christ and are viewed in Him rather than in themselves.' It is the perfect robe of Christ's righteousness that is seen by God and not the filthy rags of our sin.

Our adoption as sons in the 'household of faith' (6:10) is based on a *declarative* act of God. We do not make ourselves sons by ritualized performances. It is a consequence of empty hands stretched out in faith towards Jesus Christ. Our assurance of adoption lies in what God pronounces: 'for in Christ Jesus you are all sons of God, through faith' (3:26).

## UNITY

Paul's point all along has been to stress the commonality that exists between Christian Jews and Christian Gentiles. Indeed, it has been his aim to discontinue the use of these labels altogether as unnecessary and unhelpful. He states the point explicitly: 'There is neither Jew nor Greek, there is neither slave nor free, there is neither male nor female, for you are all one in Christ Jesus' (3:28).

As adopted sons we are members of one family. Perhaps Paul is still thinking of those in Galatia who were attempting to put Gentile believers into a different camp. They may be Christians, but they are not joining in with us! God, however, intends to make one corporate community in Christ: sheep in a flock, branches of a vine, friends of one Bridegroom, stones in a temple, a new Israel. What Paul says here, he has cause to repeat in another context, where differing spiritual giftedness threatened the unity of the body:

> For just as the body is one and has many members, and all the members of the body, though many, are one body, so it is with Christ. For in one Spirit we were all baptized into one body – Jews or Greeks, slaves or free – and all were made to drink of one Spirit (*1 Cor.* 12:12–13).

One more implication needs to be made and Paul will have brought us back full circle. Having begun with Abraham (3:6) he now returns us to Abraham (3:29). His aim is to underline the unity of God's administration of grace. Jewish believers in trusting the promise made to Abraham had, in effect, been trusting in Jesus Christ; this is what the promise to Abraham signalled. And just like them, Gentiles Christians also are children of Abraham.

# 14

# *From Slavery to Sonship*

*I mean that the heir, as long as he is a child, is no different from a slave, though he is the owner of everything, ² but he is under guardians and managers until the date set by his father. ³ In the same way we also, when we were children, were enslaved to the elementary principles of the world. ⁴ But when the fullness of time had come, God sent forth his Son, born of woman, born under the law, ⁵ to redeem those who were under the law, so that we might receive adoption as sons. ⁶ And because you are sons, God has sent the Spirit of his Son into our hearts, crying, 'Abba! Father!' ⁷ So you are no longer a slave, but a son, and if a son, then an heir through God* (Gal. 4:1–7).

As we come to what many regard as the high point of the epistle, the assertion that in union with Christ we are entitled to the fullest inheritance imaginable, we need to keep in mind the context. Paul is concerned with the Christian's relationship to the law. Several issues have become muddled in the minds of the Christians in Galatia, particularly those of Jewish background.

1. Are Gentile Christians obligated to obey the 'law' of circumcision? Specifically, can they be considered *true* Christians if they remain uncircumcised? The fact that the apostles (James, John and Peter) had given to Paul 'the right hand of fellowship' in regard to Titus (an uncircumcised Gentile) seemed, at first, to have settled the issue: Gentiles were *not* obligated to be circumcised on religious grounds. To suggest otherwise would compromise the doctrine of justification by faith *alone*. Subsequently, Peter's behaviour in Antioch had thrown everything up in the air again.

2. There is *also* the issue of the acceptance of Gentile-Christians by Jewish-Christians. Though we have not agreed with those interpreters of Galatians who insist that the entire problem was the Jewish-Christian refusal to accept Gentiles within the fold, there can be no doubt that *some* may well have been entertaining such prejudice. Paul must insist that Gentile-Christians inherit to the same degree as Jewish-Christians. Indeed he has just made the point that there is no distinction any more between Jewish and Gentile Christians (3:28). There are no promises in the New Covenant made exclusively to ethnic Jews!

3. Paul has even suspected that the issue was greater than merely one's attitude to certain ceremonial (*Jewish*) laws. He has begun to suspect that the understanding of some of the way a sinner is justified is warped. Rather than 'by faith alone', Paul suspects that many in Galatia have begun to insist that 'obedience to the law' is a prerequisite to justification.

It is apparent that Paul is opposing more than just a narrow ceremonial view of the law. Even though the issue of circumcision has been the catalyst, something fundamental is amiss in the Galatians' understanding of the relationship of the law (considered *generally*) to justification.

So far, Paul has used two metaphors to help explain the purpose of the law (as far as justification is concerned): the prison warden, and the pedagogue. Now he introduces a third: 'guardians and managers' (4:2). He introduces it with the words, 'I mean' (4:1), as though he suspects that, so far, he has not yet made his point clear enough.

## INHERITANCE LAWS

Before a minor came of age, he had no legal rights at all. He was a 'child'. He might be the heir-apparent, entitled to the full rights of inheritance. But so long as he was a child, he was no different from a slave.

In the same way that Paul has likened the law to a pedagogue, charged with disciplining young men and instructing them in the ways of the world, he now compares its function to that of 'guardians and managers', charged with taking care of the young man's estate. Until 'the date set by his father' the young man could not spend a penny of his inheritance. He had no rights of his own. He was no different in effect from a slave.

Having established the picture, Paul makes three applications:

1. *The law belongs to a preparatory age.* To those Christian-Jews who were arguing that Gentile Christians need first of all to obey the law in order to be justified, in order to be accepted among the true household of faith, Paul makes a somewhat disparaging remark about the law: it belongs to the kindergarten stage of our lives! What Paul is saying is that the law enslaves us 'to elementary principles' (4:3). There may be a reference to demonic agencies or to Satan in this expression – Satan certainly knows how to use the law to impose slavery – but it is possible to interpret it as stating that the law teaches 'fundamental principles' only.

This would certainly have been offensive to Jewish-Christians in Galatia, but no more so than what Paul has already said about the Mosaic Law: that it came after the promise (3:17); that the law shows us up as sinners (3:19); that the law was incapable of bringing life (3:21); that it actually 'imprisoned' rather than liberated (3:22). To say that it only teaches mere ABCs sounds relatively benign after all that.

We need to cast an eye forward now to verse 4, and the word 'fullness'. Before we examine what Paul says here, it will help us if we realize the contrast that is being established between *partial* and *full.* The law (especially those laws currently under discussion in Galatia and Jerusalem about circumcision and food) belonged to an age that was temporary and preparatory, not to the age of fullness and completion.

2. *We belong to that period when the inheritance has been realized.* The Galatians wanted to go back to the era of 'guardians and managers' when, by faith in Jesus Christ, they had graduated to full inheritance! What has been brought about in the coming of Jesus Christ into the world, and our subsequent faith in him, is our translation from slavery to legal inheritance. The change is *as*

*dramatic as that.* We receive *adoption as sons* in union with Christ (4:5; see also *Rom.* 8:15, 23).

Christians are 'sons of God.' It is among the most sublime things the New Testament tells us, the highest privilege of our redemption. Paul brings us now to the experiential and psychological reality of our union with Jesus Christ by faith. What the doctrine of justification by faith *alone* secures is the assurance of our sonship, our entitlement to all the inheritance that belongs to a legal heir. Thus we can say, with the *Heidelberg Catechism*:

QUESTION 1. What is your only comfort in life and in death?
ANSWER. That I with body and soul, both in life and death, am not my own, but belong unto my faithful Saviour Jesus Christ; who, with his precious blood, has fully satisfied for all my sins, and delivered me from all the power of the devil; and so preserves me that without the will of my heavenly Father, not a hair can fall from my head; yea, that all things must be subservient to my salvation, and therefore, by his Holy Spirit, He also assures me of eternal life, and makes me sincerely willing and ready, henceforth, to live unto him.

How should the word 'son' (Greek, *huios*) be translated? 'So you are no longer a slave, but a son, and if a son, then an heir through God' (4:7). In Paul's day, and until two centuries ago, inheritance rights belonged only to sons (*not* daughters!). Calling us 'sons' conveys the point in a way that was fully understood. (Incidentally, the gender issue arises in reverse when the church is called the 'bride' of Christ rather than, say, 'spouse'.)

3. *We have the Holy Spirit in our hearts.* The witness of the Spirit is related to the cry that issues from our hearts: 'Abba! Father!' It is impossible to understand this passage independently of another of similar import:

For you did not receive the spirit of slavery to fall back into fear, but you have received the Spirit of adoption as sons, by whom we cry, 'Abba! Father!' The Spirit himself bears witness with our spirit that we are children of God, and if children, then heirs – heirs of God and fellow heirs with Christ, provided we suffer with him in order that we may also be glorified with him (*Rom.* 8:15–17).

The activity of crying 'Abba! Father!' as described here in Galatians 4 is something the believer does. In the parallel passage in Romans 8, it is something the Holy Spirit does in and through the believer. There is no need to stress any tension between these two points of view. Both are true. As is so often the case in the New Testament, an activity that is deemed our responsibility is also said to be the work of God (see, for example, *Phil.* 2:12–13).

Several things are worth noting here:

1.   It should be noted that the cry, 'Abba! Father!' is one which Jesus himself uttered in the agonizing moments of Gethsemane (*Mark* 14:36). In echoing these words, we not only enter into the prayer language of Jesus, but we also identify ourselves (or rather, Jesus identifies himself) with the most intense feelings known to mankind.

In the darkest possible moments, we may use the most intimate language of communion with God, knowing him even at such times (or especially at such times!) as our Father. Paul, in Romans 8:15, uses the verb, 'cry' (*krazein*) which has onomatopoeic properties, expressive of the deepest feelings of intensity. It is the word employed of the screaming of the Gerasene demoniac (*Mark* 5:5), the yelping of the epileptic boy (*Mark* 9:26), and the cries of blind Bartimaeus (*Mark* 10:47-48) and of Jesus upon the cross (*Matt.* 27:50).

2.   When Paul goes on to say that the Spirit testifies with our spirit that we are God's children he means that our crying 'Abba! Father!' is the Spirit's work, and the evidence of his presence and of our adoption. In moments of crisis, the Spirit reminds us of our relationship with Jesus in his darkest moments. At the very least, this reminder tells us: 'He has been in this darkness, too!' At its most sublime, it assures us that nothing can ever tear apart the relationship we have with God as adopted sons.

3.   By calling the Spirit, 'the Spirit of his Son', Paul is employing the most intimate of all language. It conveys more than the idea that the Spirit gives witness to the Son. That is true. The Holy Spirit is Christ's personal representative agent. His work is to give witness to us of Christ: 'He will bear witness about me' (*John* 15:26). But Paul's meaning here is more likely to be that the Spirit belongs to the Son. He is the Son's Spirit. The Spirit knows the Son as no other knows the Son and it is precisely this Spirit who is sent into our hearts. Who better to witness of our relationship in the Father's family than the one who knows the Son so well? It is the measure of our adoption that we are reckoned as heirs in the same family as Jesus Christ – our elder brother (see also *Rom.* 8: 29).

## BORN OF A WOMAN

At the heart of Paul's pronouncement of our adopted status is a description of the One by whom this redemption from slavery and bondage is effected – Jesus, 'born of a woman, born under the law' (4:4). Once again, several things are worth noting:

1.   Paul gives expression to the existence of Jesus Christ *before* his coming into the world. God 'sent' him. His appearance in this world was preceded by the conscious activities of 'One who sends' and 'One who is sent'. He already had an existence prior to his appearance in Bethlehem. It was a movement from 'riches to rags': 'For you know the grace of our Lord Jesus Christ, that though he was rich, yet for your sake he became poor, so that you by his poverty might become rich' (*2 Cor.* 8:9).

2.   Jesus had been God's Son *eternally*. He was sent forth *as* God's Son. He did not become the 'Son of God' at the point of his incarnation. He always was the Son of God. Paul's use of this title here suggests that this expression was well known in the church from its earliest times. The Son had known communion with his Father in heaven before his appearance in human form on earth.

3.   It is often remarked that Paul has nothing to say about the virgin birth of Jesus. But there is at least a hint here. The language Paul

uses here is somewhat unusual. He uses a word *genomenos*, 'become', (used also in Romans 1:3 and Philippians 2:7). He 'became' of a woman. Paul's point is to emphasize Christ's humanity. Jesus became a real man. But Paul describes this in a way that highlights the way he came, or 'became.' At the threshold of his earthly existence, there was something different (*unique*) about him!

4. There is the language of *substitution* here. The One who was a Son became a slave in order that those who were slaves might become sons.

5. The coming of Jesus marked the great change in the calendar of redemption. The 'fullness of the times' marks the turning point from expectation to fulfilment and culmination. After this appearance, the next great event on the calendar is the second coming and the end. His coming marks the inauguration of the 'last days' (*Acts* 2:17; *Heb.* 1:2). The whole of the Old Testament was a preparation for and expectation of this moment.

6. '*Born under the law.*' It is of the deepest significance that Jesus Christ should come under the obligation of the law in all its minute detail if he were to become the representative of his people. Thus we see him circumcised on the eighth day; he lived his life in compliance with the *Torah*. The King of the universe is made subject to its demands in all its ceremonial, civil and moral components. The Ruler of all becomes a servant, without rights of his own.

But there is more than this. He not only comes under the law's demands; he comes under its condemnation. As the divine substitute, he takes the curse of the law upon himself. 'Christ redeemed us from the curse of the law by becoming a curse for us – for it is written, "Cursed is everyone who is hanged on a tree"' (3:13).

# 15

## Knowing and Being Known

*Formerly, when you did not know God, you were enslaved to those that by nature are not gods. ⁹ But now that you have come to know God, or rather to be known by God, how can you turn back again to the weak and worthless elementary principles of the world, whose slaves you want to be once more? ¹⁰ You observe days and months and seasons and years! ¹¹ I am afraid I may have laboured over you in vain* (Gal. 4:8–11).

K nowing God and knowing ourselves are, from one point of view, what the gospel is all about. Jesus expressed it in this way in the intimacy of his prayer to his heavenly Father in the closing moments of his earthly life: 'And this is eternal life, that they know you the only true God, and Jesus Christ whom you have sent' (*John* 17:3).

This forms the distinguishing feature of both Old and New Covenants. Jeremiah prophesied that the New Covenant would be a time when, 'no longer shall each one teach his neighbour and each his brother, saying, "Know the Lord," for they shall all know me, from the least of them to the greatest' (*Jer.* 31:34). He is not suggesting that saints in the Old Testament did not know the Lord! Rather, his point is that under the old economy the way into God's presence was secured by human mediators (prophets and priests). In the New Covenant, every believer shares in the prophetic anointing (*1 John* 2:20, 27). In Christ, every Christian shares in both priestly and kingly activities (*Rev.* 1:6; 5:10; 20:6). As prophets, priests and kings in union with *the* Prophet, Priest and King – the

Lord Jesus – New Covenant believers have a directness of approach, they *'know'* God, to a degree that surpasses their Old Covenant counterparts. Knowing God is what New Testament Christianity is (*Eph.* 1:17–19; *Phil.* 3:8–11; *2 Tim.* 1:12)!

So far in this section, which began with the first verse of chapter 4, Paul has been trying to make his argument clear: under the law – that is, under the Old Covenant – they were like children. They were under 'guardians and managers' until such time as they would inherit. Paul has been thinking not only of the rigorous ceremonial aspects of the law and their detailed prescriptions, but also of the law generally. Until the full reality of Christ dawned, it was all too possible to view the law wrongly – as something wholly negative and restrictive. Indeed, Paul may even have been thinking of Satan (this may be what lies behind the phrase 'elementary principles' in 4:3 and repeated again in verse 9). Satan knows how to employ the law so as to inflict bondage.

Paul's point has been that the Spirit of adoption (the 'Spirit of his Son', 4:6) has brought them into liberty. They have reached the point of inheritance through what the Spirit has done – bringing them to embrace Jesus Christ by faith.

Now Paul appeals to their experience in Christ. There is a 'formerly' (verse 8) in contrast to a 'but now' (verse 9). Their conversion from Judaism to Christianity has involved a transformation from a *'what I used to be'* to a *'what I am now'*. Paul now asks them: Why do you want to return to what you used to be?

## IGNORANCE AND IDOLATRY

Two things characterized their former life outside of Christ:

1.  They did not know God (4:8a).

2.  They were slaves to idolatry, aided in their rebellion by demonic powers. Formerly, they were slaves to 'those who by nature are not gods' (4:8b). The Galatians were in bondage to beings which they called *gods*. In denying their status as 'gods', Paul does not deny the existence of these beings. He only denies that they have a nature that qualifies them to be called gods.

Something similar is said in 1 Corinthians 8, 'For although there may be so-called gods in heaven or on earth – as indeed there are many "gods" and many "lords" – yet for us there is one God, the Father, from whom are all things and for whom we exist, and one Lord, Jesus Christ, through whom are all things and through whom we exist' (*1 Cor.* 8:5-6). In other words, though he believes there is only one God, Paul admits that other *so-called* 'gods' or 'lords' do exist. Later in the same epistle, he makes clear that these beings are demons (*1 Cor.* 10:20).

Paul's initial dealings with the Galatians had uncovered a history of worshipping pagan deities. In Lystra, a city in Galatia, God healed a crippled man through Paul (*Acts* 14: 8–18). The people of the area were so astonished at this miracle that they supposed Barnabas and Paul, whom they called Zeus and Hermes (verse 12), to be pagan gods! They wanted to sacrifice to them, and would have, if the apostles had not stopped them (verses 13–18). The Galatians were generally superstitious and worshipped pagan deities.

But Paul has something more subtle in mind. Before their conversion, these Gentiles Galatians had not known the true God, but had been enslaved to demons. The danger they were facing now as new Christians is that they might turn back and become enslaved again after having tasted the joy and freedom of Christ. Paul is concerned that this new-found liberty might be lost again by an unthinking submission, because of the pressure of the Judaizers, to what he calls 'the elementary principles of the world' (4:9).

## BEGGARLY ELEMENTS

The words translated, 'the elementary principles of the world', have been variously understood. The RSV, for example, renders the expression as the 'weak and beggarly elemental spirits'. The KJV has 'weak and beggarly elements'. The NIV has 'weak and miserable principles'. And the NASB has 'weak and worthless elemental things'. This reflects in part an ambivalence as to what exactly is being referred to. Was it something like the ABCs or elementary *principles* (as the ESV text seems to indicate), or something more sinister: spiritual (evil) beings ('elemental spirits') standing between us and God, thwarting our every endeavour?

Also, what were the 'days, months, seasons and years' that Paul criticizes the Galatians for observing? It is tempting to think of these as the Old Testament holy days. But it is unlikely that the apostle would ever refer to these holy days that God had instituted as 'weak and beggarly elements', or 'worthless elementary principles'. Paul had too much respect for the law to speak of it in this way. These Gentile converts had never observed these Jewish holy days in any case!

If Paul has Gentile Christians in mind, it is evident that the 'days, months, seasons and years' referred to in verse 10 were the pagan, idolatrous festivals and observances that the Galatian Gentiles had observed before their conversion. What they are in danger of here is turning back to their old, heathen way of life that included keeping various superstitious holidays connected to the worship of pagan deities. However, if Paul is thinking of Jewish Christians, then something more subtle is in view.

The connection between verses 9 and 10 suggests that the Galatians are returning, not to evil spirits, but to law, whether pagan or part-Jewish. This would imply that these words should be seen as references to 'elemental *things*' rather than to 'elemental *beings*'.

However, verse 8 seems to hint in the very opposite direction. The Galatians had at one time been captive to divine pretenders – though Paul emphatically denies that they are gods. What are these if not powers of evil in the heavenly realms, which Paul warns us to be on our guard against (*Eph.* 6:12)? The Galatians had been slaves of Satan's minions.

These two ideas are not mutually exclusive. Satan knows all too well how to employ the law in legalistic fashion. He knows how to enslave and cause to stumble. Behind the Judaizers' claims lay the voice of Satan! This is why Paul fears he may have laboured in vain among them (4:11), repeating a fear he had expressed in the previous chapter: 'Did you suffer so many things in vain – if indeed it was in vain?' (3:4). The danger is that they begin to use the law of God as a divine job description to help them demonstrate their moral accomplishment before God in the hope of obtaining the wages of blessing. Paul fears legalism: a return to the idea that somehow, by their obedience, they could merit the salvation of God.

## THE FINGERPRINTS OF SATAN

What Paul has done in these few verses is audacious. He has suggested, however guardedly, that behind this spiritual heresy in Galatia lay the fingerprints of Satan. In bringing them into bondage to ceremonial law, Satan has managed to convince them that they are acting on behalf of God. He has sold them a lie: that in their obedience, as they see it, they are doing something that pleases God.

The Judaizers – rigorous, moral monotheists that they were – must have been thunderstruck to hear Paul say to the Gentiles: if you begin to use the Jewish law to show God the merit of your virtue, you come under the sway of demons and are no better off than you were in your former idolatry.

Thus Paul has exposed a typical device of Satan: he drives us from carelessness to a rigorous effort of commandment and law-keeping. But such obedience is just as damning as licence. It may have all the trappings of morality and religion, but it comes from the darkest pits of hell. Be aware of that. And be warned!

# 16

## *Christ Formed in You!*

*Brothers, I entreat you, become as I am, for I also have become as you are. You did me no wrong. [13] You know it was because of a bodily ailment that I preached the gospel to you at first, [14] and though my condition was a trial to you, you did not scorn or despise me, but received me as an angel of God, as Christ Jesus. [15] What then has become of the blessing you felt? For I testify to you that, if possible, you would have gouged out your eyes and given them to me. [16] Have I then become your enemy by telling you the truth? [17] They make much of you, but for no good purpose. They want to shut you out, that you may make much of them. [18] It is always good to be made much of for a good purpose, and not only when I am present with you, [19] my little children, for whom I am again in the anguish of childbirth until Christ is formed in you! [20] I wish I could be present with you now and change my tone, for I am perplexed about you* (Gal. 4:12–20).

Something happens here that we have not been expecting. Paul suddenly adopts a very personal approach, sounding as though his feelings have been hurt by the behaviour of the Galatians. His words at this point are full of pathos. He uses the term *brothers* (verse 12). He is appealing to them on the most personal of levels – on the basis of their former respect for him. The Galatians had welcomed him into their midst 'as an angel of God', but things have grown sour since then. 'Have I then become your enemy?' he asks. What is going on here?

Such is the (supposed) abruptness of the change in tone at this point that some interpreters suggest that Paul has lost control of the argument and has yielded instead to an emotional (irrational) appeal to loyalty. However, such a view misses the point of what Paul has been doing. He has just reminded the Galatians of what they had been *before* their conversion ('formerly', 4:8). Now he is asking them to remember how things were between Paul and them *before* the Judaizers poured doubt on the apostle's theology. They were now turning back (4:9), and Paul is urging them, rather, to turn around again and become 'as I am' (4:12).

'Become as I am' says Paul, 'for I also have become as you are' (verse 12). He makes similar appeals in other letters too (*1 Cor.* 4:16; 11:1; *Phil.* 3:17; *1 Thess.* 2:14). Is this a piece of conceit on the apostle's part? Is it a resort to too high an opinion of himself and his importance? Are we not accustomed to say, 'Don't follow me, follow Christ!'

The fact that he appeals to them as *brothers* in verse 12 indicates that he still thinks of himself as *one of them* and not in some elite category *above them*. How, then, can he appeal to them to become like him?

The answer lies in Paul's understanding of the believer's union with Jesus Christ (1:22; 2:4, 16, 20; 3:14, 26, 28; 5:6). Salvation means becoming *like* Jesus Christ (*Rom.* 8:29; *2 Cor.* 3:18). Paul is saying, in effect: become like me *to the extent that* I now, by the grace of God, reflect something of Jesus Christ. Indeed he says (verse 14) that the Galatians had welcomed him into their midst 'as Christ Jesus'! This requires some explanation.

Paul is not suggesting that the Galatians had actually thought he was Jesus Christ. True, they had welcomed him as 'an angel of God' (though the word 'angel' can also be rendered 'messenger'). In Lystra, Barnabas had been welcomed as the god *Zeus* and Paul as the 'messenger' of the gods, *Hermes*. The apostles were forced to cry out, 'We also are men, of like nature with you' (*Acts* 14:15). But there is no evidence that they had mistaken him for Jesus! What Paul is suggesting is that they had received him as they would have received Jesus. He received the same honour as they would have given to the Lord Jesus himself! They saw Jesus-likeness in Paul. Paul's appeal that they become 'like him' is meant to be an appeal for Jesus-likeness.

The Galatians had nothing by way of a New Testament to help them learn what godliness looked like. No Gospels, no letters of Paul or John – only this letter that Paul is now writing. How could Paul best convey to them the shape of Christlikeness other than by saying, 'Be like me, as I am like Jesus'? What may sound to us, from our vantage point, as excessive megalomania, made perfect sense in that early setting. We are often reluctant to draw attention to ourselves – not out of constraints of modesty so much as a haunting realization that our sanctification is so pitifully *un*Christlike and immature. Our recoil at Paul's audacity may be the protection of guilt due to our lack of Christian growth and maturity.

There may be another aspect to the Galatian welcome of the apostle 'as Christ Jesus'. Paul may well have reminded them of Jesus, as to what they knew of his physical condition. Although chronologically it is possible that some of the Galatians had seen Jesus (his crucifixion would have occurred some twenty years earlier), in all likelihood they had not. But their impressions of Jesus would have been of a man accustomed to suffering. There was something about Paul that reminded them of this. The apostle came into the region of Galatia with the marks of suffering, a 'bodily ailment' (verse 13). 'My condition was a trial to you' (verse 14).

It seems most likely that Paul is alluding to some kind of disease, or temporary sickness from which he was suffering during this period – what he calls a 'bodily ailment'. He may have picked it up in Cyprus. There are some clues in this letter as to what form this sickness took.

The mention of the fact that the Galatians did not react with scorn or disdain implies that it was potentially repulsive. The fact that the Galatians were prepared to gouge out their eyes and give them to him (verse 15) suggests that Paul may well have been suffering from a disease that rendered him visually impaired. This is supported later when he says in closing the letter, 'See with what large letters I am writing to you with my own hand' (6:11). Is the apostle saying that he had had to write in large letters because he could not see to write in small ones? All this made the apostle appear ill, disfigured in some way, 'a man of sorrows', we might say. And it reminded them of Jesus. But that was *then*, as they say, and things are different now.

## WHAT HAPPENED?

Where had this kindness and affection that they had shown to the apostle gone? What had happened to their generosity, their self-denial, their expressions of love for him? Why had Paul suddenly become their 'enemy' (verse 16)?

The answer to these questions lies in the activity of the agitators in Galatia whom the apostle does not now name but simply says, 'They make much of you' (verse 17). Who are they?

- *They* are the ones encouraging the Galatian Christians to turn to a different gospel (1:6).
- *They* are the ones who have bewitched the Galatian Christians to look to the 'flesh' as the means of their justification (3:3).
- *They* are the ones who are insisting that a difference still exists in Christ between Jew and Gentile, requiring that Gentiles become Jewish in order to be fully justified (3:28).
- *They* are the ones encouraging the Galatians to return to the ABCs – kindergarten – even though they had tasted the freedom of 'life away from home'. Such a return was, for the apostle, akin to going back into slavery having once tasted emancipation (4:9).
- *They* are the ones trying 'to shut [the Galatians] out' (4:17).

But what were they trying to shut them out *of*? It is just here that interpretations of Galatians (and Paul generally) diverge. It might be helpful to outline briefly the various answers to this question as a way of demonstrating different perspectives on Paul's theology.

1. One possibility is that Paul is thinking of the analogy of slavery and liberty that had preceded this section (4:1–7, 8–11). The Galatians had tasted freedom but were now back in bondage again, whether that bondage was to the law *as a means of justification* (which is an impossibility), or to the ceremonial aspects of Judaism (some biblical and some derived from Jewish tradition). Either way, they were no longer allowed to roam freely in the terrain of God's sons. They were shut out from the true liberty that belongs to the children of God.

2. More recently, the new perspective on Paul has emphasized the hostility, endemic among Jewish-Christians at this stage in New Testament history, to the idea that a Gentile could be included as 'one of them' *without* the need for circumcision or ceremonial obedience. The agitators are shutting out *Gentiles* from the fold of Christendom unless, first of all, they are circumcised and make a promise to follow Jewish ceremonial regulations. The whole problem in Galatia is one of *inclusion* and *exclusion* and the Gentiles are being excluded, 'shut out'. This view, as we have seen, while not altogether astray in the context of the argument in Galatia, has been taken much further by some, so that they interpret almost everything, including the nature of justification itself, from this perspective.

3. The view that makes most sense in this passage is the one that understands the agitators as trying to exclude them (the Galatian Christians) from having fellowship with him (Paul). Such an interpretation ties in with the very personal (and emotional) way Paul has been phrasing things in the preceding verses. They were trying to shut them out of fellowship with the apostle so that they might 'make much of them [the agitators]' (verse 17). According to this view, a contrast is being established between making much of the apostle and making much of the agitators. Another suitor is appealing for the affections of the Galatians. This is a love-triangle, and Paul has been jilted for another!

Now that Paul is no longer with them, they are being seduced by another's attentions. And Paul wants their affection, 'not only when I am present with you', but also when he was not (verse 18). The true test of any relationship often occurs when two people are apart from each other.

This latter view is corroborated by the tone of Paul's final words in this section. Once more he appeals to their affections. He calls them 'my little children', as a mother or father might do. After all, Paul had been the instrument by which they had become children of God! He had been there at their birth to new life and freedom. And Paul uses the most intimate language of all: that of a *mother* giving birth: 'I am again in the anguish of childbirth until Christ is formed in you!' (verse 19).

The metaphor is complex! Three issues are clear, however:

*Christ Formed in You! (4:12–20)*

First, Paul loves these Galatians immensely. He may be at his wit's end, 'perplexed' by what is going on among them, hurt by the ambivalence of their love for him. But far more than that, they are brothers – children (the metaphors get mixed in the sea of emotions). He feels a responsibility towards them of a maternal kind – and nothing is stronger than that!

Second, what he longs for most of all is their *Christlikeness*, here rendered as 'Christ being formed in you' (verse 19). We are born so that we may be a new creation in Christ. He is born in us, dwells in us by his Spirit, so that we live *for* him. It was not *little Pauls* that the apostle wanted to see in Galatia, but *Christians who reflected Jesus Christ*. The pastor's heart of the apostle is thereby revealed.

Third, it is as though the apostle regarded these Galatian Christians as mere embryos, not yet fully born; fragile and delicate and in need of his protection. He wishes he could be with them.

There beats the heart of Christian Paul!

# 17

# Hagar

*Tell me, you who desire to be under the law, do you not listen to the law?* <sup>22</sup> *For it is written that Abraham had two sons, one by a slave woman and one by a free woman.* <sup>23</sup> *But the son of the slave was born according to the flesh, while the son of the free woman was born through promise.* <sup>24</sup> *Now this may be interpreted allegorically: these women are two covenants. One is from Mount Sinai, bearing children for slavery; she is Hagar.* <sup>25</sup> *Now Hagar is Mount Sinai in Arabia; she corresponds to the present Jerusalem, for she is in slavery with her children.* <sup>26</sup> *But the Jerusalem above is free, and she is our mother.* <sup>27</sup> *For it is written,*

> *'Rejoice, O barren one who does not bear;*
> *break forth and cry aloud, you who are not in labour!*
> *For the children of the desolate one will be more*
> *than those of the one who has a husband.'*

<sup>28</sup> *Now you, brothers, like Isaac, are children of promise.* <sup>29</sup> *But just as at that time he who was born according to the flesh persecuted him who was born according to the Spirit, so also it is now.* <sup>30</sup> *But what does the Scripture say? 'Cast out the slave woman and her son, for the son of the slave woman shall not inherit with the son of the free woman.'* <sup>31</sup> *So, brothers, we are not children of the slave but of the free woman* (Gal. 4:21–31).

'Now this may be interpreted allegorically' (verse 24). The expression needs some careful handling – giants have stumbled here! Some bizarre interpretations of the Bible have emerged through employing allegorical methods of interpretation.

Just as beauty is in the eye of the beholder, so also, with allegory as the interpretive method, meaning is in the eye of the most inventive!

Perhaps showing some nervousness at this point, the NIV renders the word 'figuratively'. Prior to the Reformation of the sixteenth century, it was common to employ the medieval *quadriga* by which every passage of Scripture was interpreted at four different levels: the *literal*, the *moral*, the *allegorical* and the *anagogical* (or mystical). The Reformers re-introduced rules of interpretation that focused on the meaning of words according to the rules of grammar and syntax, giving consideration to the period of history when they were written.

Essentially, an allegory is a story in which each element represents something beyond itself. Scripture employs allegory only sparingly. Apart from this story of Sarah and Hagar, the only other use made of allegory is in Paul's reference to Israel's escape from Egypt as an allegory of Christian experience (*1 Cor.* 10:1–6).

Before we consider Paul's use of allegory here we need to pick up the argument at verse 21. Paul is back to the problem at Galatia once more; this time defining it as an issue relating to the *law*. He uses 'law' over thirty times in the course of this letter and has done so over two dozen times already. One way or another, Galatians has to do with the *law*.

Paul is now rounding off the argument which began in verse 12, 'Brothers, I entreat you.' That entreaty had been followed by a very personal plea indeed, but Paul now returns to his theological and scriptural argument, one that picks up the theme of 'slavery *versus* freedom' which had been introduced in this chapter's opening verse. The Galatians were desiring 'to be under the law' (verse 21). Evidently, since they were only *desiring* this, they had not yet completely apostatized from the faith. He uses the word *law* again, in the *same* verse, 'Do you not listen to the law?'; and then goes on to cite from Genesis the story of Abraham and his two sons, Isaac and Ishmael. By *law* here he means *Scripture as a whole*, or at the very least, the *Torah* (the five books of Moses). Clearly, that is not what he meant by the first use in the verse of the word *law*.

Before we ask what Paul meant by 'under the law' in the first part of verse 21, it will be well to notice some things that Paul accomplishes in these verses. First, he raises the figure of Abraham once more. This is the eighth time he has mentioned Abraham. Since the agitators in Galatia were, on one level at least, proclaiming their Jewishness and insisting on obedience to Jewish ceremonial laws as something necessary for justification, for Paul to appeal to the father-figure of Judaism, was to take the ground from under them.

Second, by arguing from Scripture (rather than tradition), Paul is teaching them a fundamental lesson of the Christian life: it is shaped by what the Bible teaches not by the proclivities of cultic movements or leaders. Paul was not insisting on *The Teachings of Paul*, even though he was an apostle and could easily have appealed to his own authority – as he had done in the first half of this letter.

## ABRAHAM

We need to return to the argument in chapter 3 if we are going to make sense of the reference to Abraham here in chapter 4. Paul has already established that Abraham was justified by grace through faith (apart from any consideration of the law): 'For if the inheritance comes by the law, it no longer comes by promise; but God gave it to Abraham by a promise' (3:18). The apostle is now going to establish that the chosen line that followed Abraham was also based on the principle of grace. This he will do by telling the story of how Isaac was chosen above Ishmael. Hereditary linkage to Abraham avails nothing when it comes to membership in the kingdom of God. As Jesus would say to Nicodemus – another son of Abraham according to the flesh – 'Truly, truly, I say to you, unless one is born again he cannot see the kingdom of God' ( *John* 3:3).

We would probably never read the Hagar-Sarah/Ishmael-Isaac story this way had Paul not told it in the way he does here. Perhaps the agitators in Galatia were constantly referring to Abraham's family in some way. Nor is it too difficult to imagine how they might have argued. True children of God could trace their lineage back to Abraham through Isaac (the legitimate son). The Gentiles (Ishmael's heirs) could become heirs only by associating themselves with Abraham's true seed by the recognized ritual – circumcision! Surely, there must have been arguments of this nature circulating in both Galatia and Jerusalem.

Abraham had eight sons in all, six by Keturah whom he married after Sarah's death (*Gen.* 25:1–2). Only two of them are relevant to Paul's point here: Ishmael (born to Hagar, an Egyptian slave attached to Abraham's house), and Isaac (born to Sarah, Abraham's legitimate wife and a free-woman).

The point Paul wants to emphasize is that the birth of Isaac was the result of a promise which God had made, in circumstances that completely ruled out anything that either Abraham or Sarah were capable of in and of themselves. They were, after all, one hundred, and ninety years old, respectively!

The birth of Ishmael, on the other hand, was the result of human connivance – an act of disbelief in God's promise and an attempt to take matters into their own hands. In other words: Isaac was the result of an act of mercy on God's part, whereas Ishmael was the result of human contrivance and effort. One was the result of grace; the other was the result of effort.

By introducing this story, Paul has managed to bring to the surface the different strategies toward justification operating in Galatia: the way of grace through faith; the way of human effort and contrivance.

## HIDDEN MEANINGS

The story actually has six sets of twos in it: two women (mothers), two sons, two covenants, two mountains, two cities and two conditions.

| | |
|---|---|
| *Two mothers* | Sarah; Hagar |
| *Two sons* | Isaac; Ishmael |
| *Two covenants* | Abrahamic; Mosaic |
| *Two mountains* | Zion; Sinai |
| *Two cities* | Heavenly Jerusalem; Earthly Jerusalem |
| *Two conditions* | Freedom; Bondage |

In the line down from Hagar, the bond-woman, there are only children that are members of the earthly Jerusalem. Like her, they are slaves to this world, shut out from any possibility of entry into the heavenly Jerusalem.

A word of explanation is needed about the identity of the two covenants. One is said to be 'Mount Sinai' (verse 24) and therefore an allusion to the provisions of the covenant made with Moses. But what is the other covenant? Some have thought the contrast is between the Old and New Covenants, but the connection with Sarah and Isaac surely argues for it to be the covenant made with Abraham. We need to be careful, however, in drawing a contrast between Abraham and Moses, and it is easy to slip into a dispensational mindset in which the terms of salvation in the time of Abraham are seen as different from those in the time of Moses. It is important therefore to stress that the way of salvation is the same at every point in history – the time of Abraham, Moses, David, John the Baptist (the point of transition from Old to New Covenant), or of the New Testament church!

At the same time, however, we need to note an aspect of the covenant at Sinai (with Moses) that highlights an area of conflict with the covenant made with Abraham. In other words, there are areas of *continuity* and *discontinuity* between the Abrahamic and Mosaic covenants. In some ways, this is what Galatians is all about!

Having said all that, there is a sense also in which Paul sees the Abrahamic covenant and the way in which it was established as reflecting what is essential to the New Covenant – the principle of grace. Whatever positive functions the covenant with Moses had (and it did have a positive role in shaping the lives of God's people), there was a large part of it which played a role in illustrating to the people their intrinsic bondage. And Paul's point has been to say, 'You are no longer a slave, but a son' (4:7). He will repeat it again at the conclusion of the chapter, 'So, brothers, we are not children of the slave but of the free woman' (4:31). Christians are children of promise!

This is why Sarah – the barren woman of ninety – is encouraged to rejoice. Paul cites Isaiah 54:1 to that effect (though Isaiah does not explicitly make reference to Sarah).

## CITIZENSHIP OF HEAVEN

But what did Paul mean by saying of the earthly Jerusalem, 'She is in slavery with her children' (4:25)? Was Paul thinking of the Roman soldiers stationed in Jerusalem, even as he wrote? Probably not, since he is thinking in spiritual rather than secular terms. Was he, then, thinking of Jews in Jerusalem (and elsewhere) who had failed to believe in Jesus as the Messiah and were, in effect, still in slavery? Or was he thinking of Jewish Christians in the Jerusalem church? They appeared to some extent still to be 'enslaved' to Old Testament rituals and codes now made redundant by Jesus Christ's work on the cross. They had after all convinced Peter and Barnabas in Antioch that they should no longer eat with Gentile Christians! Their behaviour was no different from the response of unbelieving Jews! Since the agitators in Galatia were probably making a great deal of their connection with the church in Jerusalem (rather than with Paul and the church in Antioch), Paul is demolishing this line of argument.

What is more, Paul suggests that those advocating the theology of Hagar have no place in the Christian Church. A theology of grace and a theology of works (this is the essence of the contrast that he is making) cannot live in harmony together. Like Abraham's two wives, the tension is unbearable. One has to go, and Paul is insisting that it be Hagar and her children (verse 30, citing *Gen.* 21:10).

Our citizenship is in heaven (*Phil.* 3:20). We are members of the *Jerusalem above* which is *free*, and is *our mother* (verse 26). To be in Christ is to experience a heavenly (and heaven*ward*) calling. It is to belong to another world.

The word *corresponds* in verse 25 comes from the world of soldiers and has to do with standing in the same line as another. Followers of Hagar march to the beat of slavery. Citizens of *Jerusalem above* march to the beat of a different drummer.

To be in Christ is to be free indeed (*John* 8:36).

# 18

# *Freedom*

*For freedom Christ has set us free; stand firm therefore, and do not submit again to a yoke of slavery.*
*² Look: I, Paul, say to you that if you accept circumcision, Christ will be of no advantage to you. ³ I testify again to every man who accepts circumcision that he is obligated to keep the whole law. ⁴ You are severed from Christ, you who would be justified by the law; you have fallen away from grace. ⁵ For through the Spirit, by faith, we ourselves eagerly wait for the hope of righteousness. ⁶ For in Christ Jesus neither circumcision nor uncircumcision counts for anything, but only faith working through love* (Gal. 5:1–6).

The words *in Christ* characterize the writings of Paul, but here the apostle warns of a viewpoint that identifies someone as 'severed from Christ'. Paul is thinking of the consequence of listening to what these agitators are saying. There is the way of 'faith' (verse 6) and there is the way of 'law' (verse 4) and these two are irreconcilable. What Paul had only hinted at earlier as 'the circumcision party' (2:12) now comes to the surface. If the main issue was justification by law (see verse 4), the specific issue was their insistence that Gentile Christians be circumcised.

The opening words of chapter 5 could well serve as the focal point of the entire letter: 'For freedom Christ has set us free.' They echo words that Jesus spoke to 'the Jews' in Jerusalem at the close of the Feast of Tabernacles, 'if the Son sets you free, you will be free indeed' ( *John* 8:36). The Jews in Jerusalem were also making much of their relationship to Abraham – 'we are offspring of Abraham' ( *John* 8:33)

– just as they were in Galatia. And Jesus' point is to insist that in reality, they are slaves. They are in bondage to their fallen condition, something which the law only further exacerbates.

Jesus is the great Liberator. His first 'sermon' in the synagogue at Capernaum included the reading from Isaiah that ends with the words, 'Today this Scripture has been fulfilled in your hearing' (*Luke* 4:21). The Scripture was taken from Isaiah 61:1–2 and included the words,

> The Spirit of the Lord is upon me,
>   because he has anointed me
>     to proclaim good news to the poor.
> He has sent me to proclaim liberty to the captives
>   and recovering of sight to the blind,
>     to set at liberty those who are oppressed,
>     to proclaim the year of the Lord's favour.

The background here is the Old Testament Year of Jubilee described in Leviticus 25. It was an outworking of the Sabbath principle: every seventh year the land was allowed to rest (no ploughing of the ground or pruning of vines), and following every *seven* sevens (*every fiftieth year*) a 'Great Sabbath Year' was held, the Year of Jubilee. In that year, following the Day of Atonement (which fell in the seventh month), no agricultural work was done, land which had been 'mortgaged' to pay off debts would be returned to its original owner, and every slave was set free. A 'loud trumpet' would be blown on the Day of Atonement of that year to be heard 'throughout all your land' signalling the release of those who were in bondage (*Lev.* 25:9).

What a joyful sound it must have been to hear the 'great trumpet' for those in bondage in Old Testament times! But Jesus came to announce a greater liberation – liberation from sin's judgment and captivity. Note the references to 'slavery' in verse 1.

## LIBERTY

*Liberty* is a sustained theme in this letter:

  – the Spirit witnesses in every Christian that they are *sons*,
    not slaves (4:6-7);

– we are sons of the *free* woman, born of promise (4:22),
– we are therefore members of the 'Jerusalem above' which is *free* (4:26),
– it is for *freedom* that Christ has set us *free* (5:1),
– 'you were called to *freedom*' (5:13).

But what exactly does Paul mean here by *freedom*? Freedom from *what*? Or from *whom*? The answer to this has already been given in part, but a summary statement is now in order.

There are at least *three* elements to this freedom:

First, *the freedom represents a discontinuity with what life was like in the Old Testament period.* Paul has already used two metaphors to describe what life under the *Old* Covenant was like, *even for true believers!* It was like being under the supervision of a *paidagôgos* (3:24) – the slave whose function was to take children to school and ensure that his charges were instructed in the fundamental principles of behaviour. They were instructed to make *men* out of these boys! It was also like having 'guardians and managers' (4:1) taking care of your estate until such time as you were old enough to inherit fully and to enjoy it (4:1, 4).

Life under the *Old* Covenant was restrictive and partial in comparison with life under the *New* Covenant. The ceremonial laws were designed to be intimidating and overpowering. Ask an eight-year old what he or she can and cannot do in school (run in the corridors, speak in class, go to the bathroom whenever one pleases!) and try applying these same rules to a college student and you will see the point! I still recall vividly throwing my school books in the air on the last day of High School. I was free! Or so I thought! I was free from what I regarded as petty rules and regulations, but I was not free from law entirely. It was time to think for myself. I was now an adult. I could vote. My opinions were as important as anyone else's. And it is this idea that Paul is now weaving into the picture of what life *in Christ* is like. It is complete as opposed to partial, adult as opposed to infantile, emancipated as opposed to restrictive.

Second, *this freedom is characterized by 'life in the Spirit.'* Paul will go on to say in the next section, 'walk by the Spirit' (5:16). He will allude to it again in verse 25, though using a different verb, 'live by the Spirit'. In the passage we are examining here, Paul identifies the Christian life as one of anticipating the future consummation 'by the Spirit' (5:5). There is something about life under the New Covenant that is marked by the activity of the Holy Spirit in a way that was not the case under the Old Covenant. It is not, as has been said before, that life under the New Covenant is lawless. Far from it. The very words 'walk by the Spirit' in verse 16 are a command! We are obligated to do this. To love God, as John keeps telling us, is to obey him: 'For this is the love of God, that we keep his commandments. And his commandments are not burdensome' (*1 John* 5:3; see also *John* 14:15; 15:10).

But those who are in Christ are, in one sense, free from the law. They are free from its *condemnation*. This is, in part, what lies behind the statement in verse 3, to the effect that obedience to the requirement of circumcision leads to other requirements also. Circumcision took place when the Jewish boy was eight days old. Thus the observance of *days* has been introduced. It does not stop with just one law. Before you know it, there are more and more laws to obey. This was exactly what had happened in Antioch when Peter and Barnabas decided to obey food laws out of respect for the issue of circumcision!

But Paul has more than *that* in view. He is thinking of what the law *does* – it condemns! The law shows us how unable we are to comply with its demands. And obedience here and there is not enough. The law is merciless. It expects total compliance at every point. What had the law done, except bring them 'under slavery' (2:4), 'under a curse' (3:10)? It brings *everything* into a prison and calls it *sin* (3:22).

That is why Paul *begins* this letter with something the Old Covenant could only anticipate from a distance, but never experience in the way the Christians in Galatia could – 'the Lord Jesus Christ who gave himself for our sins' (1:4). Never, in the long history of the Old Testament could any believer have said such words with such assurance of forgiveness and acceptance. True, the sacrifices *spoke of* Christ and *anticipated* Christ, but there would always be the need for one more sacrifice-tomorrow, next week, next month, next year ... This is why Paul will return to the cross again at the close of the letter, saying, 'But far be it from me to boast except in the cross of our Lord Jesus Christ' (6:14).

Third, *this freedom allows me to have the most intimate and open relationship with my Father in heaven.* Think about it: 'In Christ', God is my Father. I don't have to earn his love. My relationship does not depend on my obedience. That is why he says, in response to the insistence on circumcision by these agitators in Galatia, 'You are severed from Christ, you who would be justified by the law; you have fallen away from grace' (5:4). Paul is not suggesting that true Christians can fall from grace, but that this teaching destroys grace.

Seeking justification by obedience to the law (note what Paul says in verse 4) is the very opposite to grace. The relationship is legal rather than familial. The law is unforgiving and relentless. We know where we stand with our Father in heaven – *justified*! We do not have to *pretend*. He knows that we are sinners and accepts us in Christ regardless. Those who seek justification by obedience find themselves overestimating their obedience or underestimating their disobedience. There is always a basic dishonesty about the relationship. The apostle is telling the Galatians that the way of law can only lead to a distrust of God. It breeds hypocrisy and cynicism. Only a relationship based on grace can ever lead to *true* freedom.

## THE HOPE OF FAITH

One of the basic features of the New Testament's teaching on salvation, and our experience of it, is its *eschatological* nature. That is, it has a *future* perspective to it. We *are* saved, but in a sense we are *going to be* saved. We are sons, but the full experience of our sonship awaits the breaking of the next era in God's redemptive design. In verse 5, Paul gives full expression to the 'now – not yet' tension that we experience prior to 'the revealing of the sons of God' (*Rom.* 8:19). Here he puts it this way: 'For through the Spirit, by faith, we ourselves eagerly wait for the hope of righteousness.' As John will add: 'Beloved, we are God's children now, and what we will be has not yet appeared; but we know that when he appears we will be like him, because we shall see him as he is' (*1 John* 3:2).

A question arises concerning the identity of the 'we' in verse 5, 'We ourselves eagerly wait for the hope of righteousness.' The answer seems obvious: he means every true Christian as opposed to those heretics in Galatia and elsewhere who were advocating a works-based salvation. But recent interpretations insist that Paul means 'we *Jewish* Christians'. Paul's point in that case is that even we who have been circumcised do not depend on *that* for our future status, rather we depend on the new life which is ours 'by the Spirit'. If that is true of *those who have been circumcised*, how much more is it true of Gentiles who have not!

But this grants a distinction between circumcised and uncircumcised Christians that Paul is unwilling to make. In the very next verse, Paul insists that 'in Christ Jesus neither circumcision nor uncircumcision counts for anything, but only faith . . .' (verse 6). This would hardly follow (note the '*for*' at the beginning of the verse) if Paul had conceded that a distinction actually exists.

In verses 5 and 6, Paul unites three ideas that belong inseparably together: *faith, hope* and *love*. A Christian has faith in Jesus Christ, loves him and all who belong to him, and longs for the world to come.

In particular, faith manifests itself in love. It may well be that part of the problem the apostle has perceived in the agitators in Galatia is a form of racism – they had no love for Gentiles. Paul could have identified with such an attitude in his *former* life. But the Spirit has birthed a love in his heart toward those whom he had once regarded as *dogs*.

The evidence of faith (but *not* its source) is a loving disposition toward other members of the kingdom of God.

# 19

## *Love*

*You were running well. Who hindered you from obeying the truth? [8] This persuasion is not from him who calls you. [9] A little leaven leavens the whole lump. [10] I have confidence in the Lord that you will take no other view than mine, and the one who is troubling you will bear the penalty, whoever he is. [11] But if I, brothers, still preach circumcision, why am I still being persecuted? In that case the offence of the cross has been removed. [12] I wish those who unsettle you would emasculate themselves!* (Gal. 5:7–12 ).

Paul occasionally employs metaphors from the world of sports to make his point. Here the imagery is of someone 'cutting in' (NIV) and hindering a fellow-competitor's progress. There were rules in the Greek games about such things. Even if the athletic metaphor does not quite fit us, we have all experienced someone 'cutting in' when a car has pulled in in front of us causing us to slam on the brakes!

## PERSEVERANCE

We are called by God (verse 8) to a long-distance race that is beset with obstacles and hindrances. It is not a brief sprint but a marathon that will take our entire life to run. We should expect that, from time to time, we will encounter things that prevent us from running in the proper direction. It is through many tribulations that we enter the kingdom of God (*Acts* 14:22). But Paul is assured that his 'brothers' (verse 11) will ultimately persevere (verse 10). He has 'confidence' about it (verse 10).

But Paul has said some very strong things about the agitators in Galatia. They have been teaching something which can only be called heresy – a view of justification that leads him to the conclusion: 'You are severed from Christ' (5:4). How, then, can he be assured that others will not yield to this false teaching? How can he be certain that the 'spell' that has been cast upon them will not lead to their doom (see 3:1)?

The answer is that Paul's certainty does not lie *in them*, but *in the Lord* (verse 10). *He* will hold on to those whom *he* has called (see verse 8). The race may be strewn with obstacles. The pilgrim in Psalm 121 who could see that the hills *en route* to Jerusalem might be filled with potential bandits and marauders, asks, 'Where will my help come from?' 'From the Lord' was the answer given him (*Psa.* 121:1–2). It is the same answer that came to the apostle! God's covenant is the source of all our confidence. The Galatians will keep on going because God will keep them going.

## THE ONE WHO HINDERED YOU

Who exactly is troubling the Galatians? Paul refers to '*the one* who is troubling you' (verse 10), suggesting a single individual. He does not name anyone in particular. Perhaps he did not know his name, or perhaps he didn't think it appropriate to name names at this point. (He *does* name individuals elsewhere.)

• We have hinted that the 'men of James' (2:12) who came from Jerusalem were the same ones as those who were troubling the Christians in Galatia. We do not know this for sure, but it would make a great deal of sense if this were so.

• It may be that Paul did not know *exactly* who they were. He does ask, 'Who has bewitched you?' (3:1). And here he asks, 'Who hindered you?' Does this mean, especially since he says, 'the one who hindered you . . . whoever he is', that he does not know? Has Paul only heard bits and pieces, enough to be concerned, but not enough to make an identification?

- He always talks about them (or him!) in the third person. The letter is not addressed to them, but to the Christians in Galatia.

- It is possible to take note of what Paul is saying and assume that, *at every point*, the agitators in Galatia were saying the very opposite (what is sometimes called 'mirror-reading'). We cannot be certain that this was always the case. Paul may be expanding his argument in the fear that the agitators might well further develop their own viewpoint. That would be a reasonable thing for a teacher to do. But is this caution needed here, since Paul says 'he will bear the penalty' (verse 10)? He seems to be well aware of what was being said.

- The trouble in Galatia might well have been at an early stage. The quotation of a proverb in verse 9 to the effect that a little leaven leavens the whole lump suggests that.

Paul issues a word of solemn warning to the one who is hindering these Galatians. He faces the penalty, the final judgment of God.

## DID PAUL EVER PREACH CIRCUMCISION?

'But if I, brothers, still preach circumcision . . .' (5:11). Had Paul initially preached circumcision, perhaps to God-fearers in the synagogue? *Hardly!* Was this the 'lie' that was being circulated?

Paul was not simply '*anti*-circumcision.' In the case of Titus, he was emphatically opposed to it, since those who were insisting upon it seem to have regarded it as essential to justification. This led to the charge that Paul was not only anti-circumcision, but anti-law (*antinomian*) generally (see *Acts* 21:21). In Timothy's case, however, Paul agreed to circumcision. Timothy was Jewish in any case through his mother, and no such pressure (as in Titus's case) was apparent. It would be appropriate for him in his ministry to 'the circumcised' (Jews). His opponents therefore would have said things like: "Paul is an advocate of circumcision when it suits him (in Jerusalem, for example)." Or perhaps his opponents were reminding the Galatians of what Paul used to believe *before* his conversion, when he most certainly *did* 'preach circumcision.'

In 1 Corinthians 7:17–20, Paul outlines his position on circumcision very clearly. When the issue of one's acceptance before God is not at stake, Paul is indifferent to it. He regards it as more or less a badge of cultural identity.

In Galatia, where the issue of justification is very much to the fore, he desires that his opposition to the necessity of circumcision be known. Indeed, he is being persecuted for it (verse 11). This persecution would be incongruous *if*, as the folk in Galatia are being told, Paul is not really opposed to circumcision in any sense. As it is, his position on circumcision is an *offence* (stumbling block) to his opponents (verse 11).

Paul makes himself crystal clear. He adds a comment in order to underline his point – a comment which some have found both crude and rude! Try and follow his line of thought: if they regard circumcision as *necessary* for one's acceptance with God, why stop there? Why not go all the way? Why not emasculate yourself? As one translation puts it, 'Tell those who are disturbing you I would like to see the knife slip'! If the removal of foreskin helps, how much more castration!

It is confrontational. But sometimes only such confrontation gets the message across.

## 20

# *Flesh and Spirit*

*For you were called to freedom, brothers. Only do not use your freedom as an opportunity for the flesh, but through love serve one another. [14] For the whole law is fulfilled in one word: 'You shall love your neighbour as yourself.' [15] But if you bite and devour one another, watch out that you are not consumed by one another.*

*[16] But I say, walk by the Spirit, and you will not gratify the desires of the flesh. [17] For the desires of the flesh are against the Spirit, and the desires of the Spirit are against the flesh, for these are opposed to each other, to keep you from doing the things you want to do. [18] But if you are led by the Spirit, you are not under the law. [19] Now the works of the flesh are evident: sexual immorality, impurity, sensuality, [20] idolatry, sorcery, enmity, strife, jealousy, fits of anger, rivalries, dissensions, divisions, [21] envy, drunkenness, orgies, and things like these. I warn you, as I warned you before, that those who do such things will not inherit the kingdom of God* (Gal. 5:13–21).

Freedom! It serves as the key to this entire epistle. In arguing for God's way of justification, Paul is resolute: *it is not of works, and any hint that it is so is a step in the direction of bondage and slavery.*

## THE ON-GOING STRUGGLE

Having introduced the idea of the flesh in verse 13, Paul now embarks on one of the best-known sections of the epistle in which he contrasts the (way of the) flesh and the (way of the) Spirit in verses 16–21. Every Christian lives in two spheres at once: the flesh and the Spirit. On one level, a Christian lives in a new order of existence, a new dimension – in union with Jesus Christ and indwelt by the Holy Spirit. At the same time, he lives out this existence in a body that is firmly rooted in this world. The Philippians, for example, who are 'in Christ' and yet are 'at Philippi' (*Phil.* 1:1); the Corinthians, who are 'sanctified in Christ,' are also 'in Corinth' (*1 Cor.* 1:2).

The reason why Christians are not to 'gratify the desires of the flesh' is that in reality Christians are not 'in the flesh' but 'in the Spirit' (*Rom.* 8:9). Having once been in union with Adam, a Christian is now in union with Jesus Christ, 'crucified with Christ' (2:20), even though the flesh remains a force in his life, desiring what is 'against the Spirit' (verse 17). Tension exists for the believer because, on the one hand, the 'end of the ages' has dawned (*1 Cor.* 10:11), yet, on the other, he remains firmly in this sin-cursed and ultimately doomed world. The Christian lives in both the world of the resurrection and in this world at one and the same time. This results in the experience of contrary urgings within: 'For I do not do the good I want, but the evil I do not want is what I keep on doing' (*Rom.* 7:19). The Spirit maintains and enables those urgings for good (the regenerate desires). The Adamic instincts ('the flesh') while dethroned are not yet eliminated, but the Christian life is lived in a life-long determination to destroy them.

What is in view here is fundamental to a New Testament understanding of the relationship between sanctification's definitive aspect (what we now are in Christ by the Spirit) and its progressive aspect (what we desire to, and one day will, become). Paul calls us to a life of constant watchfulness and diligence in which we are to use the weapons of prayer on the one hand and mortification (killing sin) on the other (see verses 16–17; *Eph.* 5:18; *James* 1:14–15).

Specifically here in Galatians 5, the parameters of the present age are variously termed, 'the flesh', 'the desires of the flesh', and 'the works of the flesh'. However radical the transformation of the new existence in Christ may be, it has not as yet eradicated the influence of the world, dominated as it is by sin and the devil, to which the flesh is particularly susceptible. So long as this is the case, tension and conflict are the inevitable result: 'The desires of the flesh are against the Spirit, and the desires of the Spirit are against the flesh' (verse 17).

Care needs to be taken not to equate 'flesh' as Paul uses it here and elsewhere with 'physical', though clearly, there is a physical dimension in which it operates. Paul is not implying that the truly 'spiritual' (that is, non-physical) is the part of our existence that is in union with Christ, and that therefore the goal of redemption is eventually to be rid of the body entirely. Such notions did indeed exist in New Testament times, as they do in our own. But Paul's view is more complex than that. True, the works of the flesh can take physical shape, as Paul makes clear in Romans 6:13 when he exhorts his readers to offer 'the parts of [their] bodies' as 'instruments of righteousness'. But the list employed here includes such things as attitudes, motivations and inner dispositions: self-absorption, self-reliance, externalism and ritual rather than inner reality.

## THE RESOLVE

Twice (in verses 16 and 25), Paul urges his readers to 'walk by the Spirit'. But in fact Paul employs two different words. In verse 16 he uses the general word for 'walk'; but in verse 25 his word suggests the idea of marching in file with others, as for example a soldier might be called to do on a parade ground. Verse 25 could be translated, 'keep in step with the Spirit' (as it is in the NIV). We will consider verse 25 in the next chapter, but it should be noted that even here in verse 16, Paul's point is that the Holy Spirit is to be obeyed and followed *precisely*!

In verse 18, Paul throws further light on what he means by 'walking' in the Spirit. We are '*led*' by the Spirit (5:18). Since he contrasts being 'led' by the Spirit with being 'under the law' (verse 18), we might think that he is arguing for a degree of disengagement from the demands of the law. Indeed the footnote on 'under the law' in one study Bible suggests that Paul is saying we do not need to try and please God by 'minute observation of the law for salvation *or sanctification*'. But that is to misunderstand Paul and to suggest he is advocating a degree of antinomianism! After all, the list of things named which we are to mortify is a lengthy and detailed one (verses 19-21)! Rather, what Paul has in mind is the answer to the question:

What happens when I fail to win the struggle against the flesh? Will that mean my certain condemnation? His answer is: *negatively*, our acceptance (justification) does not depend on our keeping of the law; *positively*, all the help we need – both in terms of instruction and resources – comes from the Spirit. The Spirit leads us! God's own Spirit helps in the conflict with the flesh! Like the lead locomotive on a train of hundreds of carriages, the power of the Spirit is passed along to us. In our continuing struggle with ongoing sin, the reassurance of this divine resource is our great motivation.

We are not alone in this struggle!

## LISTS

Paul is never content with mere generalizations when it comes to sin. Sins have names!

The list is not exhaustive, as the expression 'and things like these' indicates (verse 21). It contains fifteen sins, which may be grouped into sub-categories of their own: sexual sins, religious sins (especially idolatry), social sins and drinking sins.

*Sexual sins.* Interestingly, and disturbingly, it begins with a list of three sexual sins: 'sexual immorality, impurity, sensuality' (verse 19). In similar lists, Paul again mentions sexual sins as primary (*1 Cor.* 6:9, 18; *Eph.* 5:5; *1 Thess.* 4:3), as does Jesus in Mark 7, where he mentions sexual immorality before theft and murder (*Mark* 7:21). It is not mere prudery that highlights sexual deviance, but something more fundamental. This is an insight into the nature of sin itself: self-gratification rather than neighbourly love. Sexual deviance of every kind (Paul uses the term 'sexual immorality' generally here) is by nature unloving – even though it is often described as 'love'. 'Impurity' and 'sensuality' highlight the defilement and lawlessness that follows in the wake of sexual sin. *Sensuality* (or 'debauchery') depicts the loss of all restraint and decency.

That these words characterize our own day as much as they did that of the apostle is worthy of note, but a further issue arises here. It would be perfectly understandable for Paul to address the world in this way, but why does he feel the need to talk to Christians this way? Surely none of the Christians in Galatia were guilty of this kind of behaviour! Probably not, but in his letter to the Corinthians just a few years later, Paul notes that some of these Christians in Corinth had *at one time* lived precisely this way (*1 Cor.* 6:11). They had been rescued by the gospel. The temptation to return would undoubtedly arise from time to time. The warning is meant to prepare them for such a demonic onslaught.

*Religious sins.* If sexual sins have as their essence self-gratification, it is easy to see why Paul next mentions 'idolatry'. It is Satan's most powerful tool and hence the association with 'sorcery' or *witchcraft*. The Greek word for sorcery (from which we derive the word *pharmacy*) implies the use of narcotics. Some have seen a connection with the use of drugs in the abortion practices of the first century.

*Sins against our neighbour.* Does this list reflect the main sins in the Galatian churches? It is difficult to distinguish between some of them (enmity and strife, dissensions and divisions, for example). Paul may well be varying expressions, thesaurus-like, to maximize the effect of what he wants to say:

> *enmity* (hatred, quarrels)
> *strife* (discord, temper)
> *jealousy*
> *fits of anger*
> *rivalries* (selfish ambition)
> *dissensions* (backbiting, bad-mouthing)
> *divisions* (factions)
> *envy* (actually in the plural here, envyings).

Were the Galatian churches already hopelessly divided? No doubt some of this was caused by the Judaizing faction because of their deep unhappiness with Paul's teaching and their eagerness to return to an earlier form of their self-styled 'orthodoxy'. The easiest way to ensure that the gospel would flounder in Galatia would be to set Christians at odds with each other so that any meaningful relationship would be out of the question. Whatever it was that they were in disagreement about, *the way they expressed it* was indefensible.

*Alcohol.* The last two items in this list both concern the abuse of alcohol: 'drunkenness' and 'orgies'. The latter may bring to mind the sexual sins at the start of the list, creating an *inclusio*, or book-end effect (common in Hebrew style). But there is more to this than literary style. The abuse of alcohol often leads to sins involving sex, and Paul is bringing us back to the point where he began his list, perhaps hinting that sin is a vicious cycle from which there is no escape apart from grace.

## HOLINESS

At the conclusion of the list Paul makes a categorical statement calculated to shock. Those who practise such sins cannot inherit the kingdom of God (verse 21). Evidently, this was something Paul had said to them during his visit to Galatia, 'as I told you before'. Is Paul suggesting, after all, that inclusion within the kingdom of God is based on our obedience to a set of rules? Hasn't he been making the point over and over again that we are not justified by anything that we do, but by faith alone in Jesus Christ alone *apart from the works of the law* (2:16; 3:2, 5)? Did he not say that any attempt to be justified by obedience to the law is cursed (3:10)? How can he now say that disobedience banishes from the kingdom?

1. Paul is *not* saying that anyone who commits one or all of these sins can never be included in the kingdom of God. For no one (certainly not the apostle himself) can say that they are innocent of all of these sins. Paul has in mind those who remain impenitent, who *continue* in these sins. There is forgiveness for every kind of transgression for those who repent and trust in the Saviour, Jesus Christ.

2. Though our justification is not based on obedience but is received by faith alone, it does not follow that those thus justified are thereby free from the necessity of obedience. We are justified by faith alone, but genuine faith is *never* alone, it is always accompanied by works! We can distinguish between justification and sanctification at this point. What Paul is saying here refers to sanctification rather than to justification. It is a statement that is aimed against easy-believism: that one can be justified and live as one pleases. No! The grace that justifies is the grace that sanctifies. There is no faith without works (*James* 2:14–26; see also *Gal.* 5:6).

3. The kingdom of God is distinguished by holiness. As the final words of the Bible make clear, nothing that is unclean may enter the eternal city – those who practise habitually the kinds of sins mentioned here are outside the gates (*Rev.* 22:15).

That's how *serious* sin is!

# *Walking in Step with the Spirit*

*But the fruit of the Spirit is love, joy, peace, patience, kindness, goodness, faithfulness, * [23] *gentleness, self-control; against such things there is no law. * [24] *And those who belong to Christ Jesus have crucified the flesh with its passions and desires.*

[25] *If we live by the Spirit, let us also walk by the Spirit.* [26] *Let us not become conceited, provoking one another, envying one another* (Gal. 5:22–26).

It is with something of a sense of relief that Paul now turns from his catalogue of fifteen sins to list the fruit of the Spirit. Before looking at the list in detail, it is interesting to note some general things that Paul teaches in this passage.

1. A sharp contrast is intended between the 'works of the flesh' and the 'fruit of the Spirit'. The first owe their origin to, and gain their energy from, the flesh. The second is a product of a power that lies outside of us. The one is the product of our activity in our fallen nature (in union with Adam). The other comes from our renewed nature (in union with Jesus Christ) through the indwelling of the Holy Spirit. It would be hard to envisage a greater contrast than that depicted by the two lifestyles described here. It highlights that those who are 'in Christ' are 'a new creation' (*2 Cor.* 5:17). This is *literally* a 'new creation'! The order of the world to come has already begun to manifest itself in the life of the believer. The contrast is between a world doomed to destruction and one which will last for ever and in which no sin resides. The believer is not yet perfect, of course.

The struggle that Paul has been relating in the previous verses between the flesh and the Spirit testifies to that. But a decisive and monumental change has already taken place.

2. The chief characteristic of holiness (displaying the fruit of the Spirit) is *Christlikeness*. Those 'who belong to Christ' (5:24) thereby fulfil 'the law of Christ' (6:2). Christians desire to be godly; they *are to be* like Christ. There is a distinction between every other community and the Christian community, and the latter is to stand apart in terms of its holiness and character.

3. The difference between the two communities (non-Christian and Christian) is that the one lives according to the flesh and the other does not. Here Paul reintroduces an idea first stated in 2:20 (and which will occur again in 6:14): Christians 'have crucified the flesh' (5:24). But there is an important difference. The verb here is active rather than passive. Whereas in 2:20 (and 6:14) the reference is to something that has been done *to us*, here at 5:24 Paul refers to what we do. Is Paul now saying that the Christian life is, after all, something for which we have to *work*?

The answer is simple, yet profound. Paul is not suggesting that something *we do* contributes to our *belonging* to Christ (verse 24). But we cannot come to belong to Christ without simultaneously abandoning the world (of the flesh) to which we formerly belonged. Trusting in the crucified Saviour always involves having the cross being laid on our shoulder. Thus, those who belong to Christ have – in a decisive way – 'crucified the flesh'.

Paul's implication is that since this is what was involved in becoming a Christian in the first place, the ongoing rejection of the 'works of the flesh' and the development of 'the fruit of the Spirit' is the only consistent life-pattern possible. Are we therefore responsible for our sanctification?

The answer to this is 'Yes' and 'No'! We *are* responsible for our sanctification, but not in the sense that we accomplish it entirely ourselves. Paul can say in Philippians 2:12 that we are to 'work out' our own salvation with fear and trembling because God is at work within us both to will and to do of his good pleasure. Just so, here in Galatians 5 we are urged to 'walk by the Spirit' (verse 25). As we noted in the previous chapter, *walk* here contains the idea of marching in file with others – and according to the urgings and guidance of another, as, for example, a soldier might be called to do on a parade ground. We are to 'keep in step with the Spirit' (NIV). This calls for a total commitment on our part in the certainty that every accomplishment is of his doing. For in the end, any accomplishment we make in this area is only of his (the Holy Spirit's) doing.

4. The dynamic of the Christian life is highlighted in these verses. We are to become what in essence we already are. On the basis of our union with Christ – we already 'belong to Christ' (think of this as *definitive* sanctification) – we are to work out our salvation according to the life-long pattern of mortification and vivification – putting sin to death and displaying the fruits of the Spirit.

## FRUITS OF THE SPIRIT

Just as Paul has given us a catalogue of sins or vices, so he now provides a catalogue of fruit. If the former list was perhaps deliberately disorderly, this one demonstrates a pleasing pattern of three groups of three. Tempting as it is to think of a trinitarian order here, it is more likely that Paul groups these graces according to these sub-categories:

Three graces demonstrating *the believer's attitude to God,*
Three graces demonstrating *the believer's attitude to*
*other people,* and
Three graces demonstrating *the believer's attitude to himself.*

## LOVE, JOY, PEACE

The first group of three begins with *love.* This seems especially relevant to Christians divided over their understanding of the gospel. If they are demonstrating a Christlike spirit, they must show love. Love is mentioned first because it is paramount. It is the chief of graces. It reflects the character of God himself: God is love (*1 John* 4:8, 16).

Paul expands on love in 1 Corinthians 13:4–8 emphasizing its total lack of self-concern. It was modelled by Jesus in the upper room in his washing of the disciples' feet. It is by such self-denying behaviour that true disciples of Jesus are recognized (*John* 13:34–35).

Paul does not specify the objects of our love. Is it love of God? Is it of our fellow-Christians? Is it of non-Christians? The answer would seem to be 'all three'!

Are we surprised that *joy* occurs so near the top of Paul's list of the fruits of the Spirit. Somehow, and erroneously, we have formed the impression that Paul was not a particularly joyful person! Certainly his tone in this epistle has bordered on the hostile! But another letter of his, Philippians, is known as 'the epistle of joy' (see *Phil.* 1:18 (twice), 25–26; 2:18; 3:1; 4:4).

The apostle Peter reminds the Christians in Pontus, Galatia, Cappadocia, Asia and Bithynia, that they are to 'rejoice with joy that is inexpressible and filled with glory' (*1 Pet.* 1:8). In fact, the word 'joy' occurs sixty-two times in the New Testament, and the word 'rejoice' over forty times.

But joy *commanded*? How can that be? Isn't joy spontaneous, arising in response to certain situations, but with no guarantee of its emergence? No! What the Spirit of Christ accomplishes within us is a reappraisal of the way our wills relate to our affections (emotions). In the Spirit, our affectional response can be 'called forth' in response to what God has revealed to us. Knowing God elicits joy. We are not at liberty to leave this fruit aside as though it were merely a matter of temperament and disposition. Every Christian is to be joyful *in the Lord*.

Paul does not specify the cause of our joy. Is it what God has done for us in Jesus Christ? Is it our current circumstances? Is it our relationship with each other in the kingdom of God? The answer would seem to be, again, 'all three'!

*Peace* echoes the familiar Hebrew greeting *shalom*, meaning both physical and spiritual well-being. It is the result of our justification by faith alone in Jesus Christ alone (*Rom.* 5:1). Having been freed from the law's condemnation and tyranny, every Christian is at peace with God. There is no fear of condemnation any more. It is the certainty that every step we take is ordered by a God who loves us and cares for us. No set of circumstances can undo what God is determined to accomplish in us. Our justification guarantees glory to come (*Rom.* 5:2; 8:30), and the knowledge of it should fill our hearts with a tranquillity that 'goes beyond our understanding' (*Phil.* 4:7).

Paul does not specify the sphere in which this peace operates. Is it in our relationship to God's holiness (justification)? Is it in the outworking of God's plan for us in our daily lives, however perplexing that may seem to be (providence)? Is it in the relationships we enjoy as brothers and sisters in the church fellowship? Again, the answer would seem to be 'all three'!

## PATIENCE, KINDNESS, GOODNESS

*Patience*, as Calvin puts it, 'is to take everything in good part and not to be easily offended'. It is often rendered 'longsuffering'. In secular literature the word was used of someone with 'a slow fuse', not easily given to rage or temper. In the New Testament it is usually associated with the idea of not being easily provoked to revenge despite wrong or injustice (*2 Cor.* 6:6; *Eph.* 4:2; *Col.* 1:11; 3:12). It is a quality that is revealed in God himself, as is the next word, kindness (*Rom.* 2:4).

*Kindness*. Christians are to be kind to one another and to clothe themselves with kindness (*Eph.* 4:32; *Col.* 3:12). Christians must not be sharp and bitter, but gentle, mild, courteous. Gentleness overlooks other people's faults and covers them up.

*Goodness*. The (Greek) word means all that is benign, soft, winning, tender, either in temper or behaviour. A person is good when he is willing to help others in their need. Since the Bible describes God's redeeming love as his 'goodness' (*Psa.* 100:5; *Mark* 10:18), it would imply that our goodness must be reflective of his divine love for sinners.

## FAITHFULNESS, GENTLENESS, SELF-CONTROL

Faithfulness, gentleness and self-control were regarded as virtues in the secular world of Paul's day. *Faithfulness* is once again an attribute of God (*Rom.* 3:3). In secular Greek it describes someone who could be trusted, who would act according to principle (in good faith). Perhaps Paul had in mind the thought that the Galatians had formerly been particularly faithful towards him (4:13–16).

*Gentleness* is a word that Jesus used to describe himself adding that he was also 'lowly in heart' (*Matt.* 11:29). It has nothing to with being wimpish and weak! Paul was neither of these! But it does mean being considerate of others and slow in asserting oneself.

*Self-control*, interestingly, was often associated with sexual matters in Paul's day – in which case the list of vices begins and the list of graces ends with the same issue. Paul has come full circle. But it need not necessarily be limited to sexual purity, and can refer to the strength to say 'no' to oneself in order to meet the needs of others. Christians are more concerned about others than they are about themselves. Like Jesus, they humble themselves (*Phil.* 2:5-8; *Rom.* 15:3).

In the end, what this list gives us is a description of Jesus Christ. What Paul describes as 'walking in the Spirit' and bearing 'the fruit of the Spirit' finds its prototype in Jesus himself. What was fully realized in Jesus as the 'last Adam' (*1 Cor.* 15:45) and 'second man' (*1 Cor.* 15:47) is now to be manifested in the lives of his people. Jesus incarnated and thereby modelled the life of fruitfulness. If we are unsure what this life looks like, all we need do is examine the life of Jesus!

## LAW IN THE HEART

One more troublesome statement needs comment – 'against such things there is no law' (verse 23). On any consideration, this is a difficult remark to understand. It belongs with a similar statement made a few verses earlier – 'if you are led by the Spirit, you are not under the law' (5:18). Is Paul suggesting, in opposition to the Judaizers in Galatia, that Christians do not live according to a legal standard any more? No, we know from what he says elsewhere, in the opening verses of Romans 6 for example, that Paul would never embrace that point of view. Many have thought that Paul was indeed suggesting something of this nature, but it runs counter to what Paul himself says in this, and every other, epistle. Christians are to obey! 'Do we then overthrow the law by this faith? By no means! On the contrary, we uphold the law' (*Rom.* 3:31).

Christians have crucified the flesh and display the fruits of the Spirit. This is not a 'take it or leave it' remark, but one which Paul clearly intends Christians to obey. He has made plain in the bluntest terms just a few verses earlier the consequences of not doing so: 'those who do such things will not inherit the kingdom of God' (5:21). Paul will give a list of things (6:16, *rule*, not merely wise advice) he intends Christians to obey, including the need to carry the burdens of others, and to not be weary in well-doing and to do good to others, especially those who belong to the household of God.

What is Paul saying? It is not to the *rule* of law as such that Paul refers, but to the *condemnation* of the law. In Christ there are no threats of condemnation (*Rom.* 5:1; 8:1). There is no 'against' heard from Sinai to those who 'belong to Christ'. A Christian is, to borrow another of the apostle's enigmatic statements, 'under the law of Christ' (*1 Cor.* 9:21).

All the law-keeping in the world without Christ and the Spirit sets us on a road that leads to death. But in Christ there is no condemnation!

## 22

# *Bearing One Another's Burdens*

*Brothers, if anyone is caught in any transgression, you who are spiritual should restore him in a spirit of gentleness. Keep watch on yourself, lest you too be tempted. ² Bear one another's burdens, and so fulfil the law of Christ. ³ For if anyone thinks he is something, when he is nothing, he deceives himself. ⁴ But let each one test his own work, and then his reason to boast will be in himself alone and not in his neighbour. ⁵ For each will have to bear his own load. ⁶ One who is taught the word must share all good things with the one who teaches* (Gal. 6:1–6).

The closing chapter of Galatians looks a little haphazard. But while parts of Galatians read like a theological tract, we must remember that Paul is writing a *letter*. As is still often the case today with letter writing, haste and brevity take over. Things are said without elaboration or connection with what has been previously written. Writing materials (or in this case, papyrus) were expensive, and perhaps there was now little room left for elaboration.

Nine times in this epistle, Paul addresses the Galatians as 'brothers' (1:11; 3:15; 4:12, 28, 31; 5:11, 13; 6:1,18). This tends to happen at points of increased emotion and pastoral concern. In a letter which has been particularly severe in places, the apostle does not want to lose all sense of proportion: whether it be theological error or, as here, a particular sin that is in view, the apostle reminds them that they have professed to be Christians and are therefore members of the family of God. It is because of this that what he is now about to raise with them is so important. Sin not only affects the person who commits it; it offends the entire family!

# DISCIPLINE

Paul now raises the possibility that a member of the church may be 'caught' in a 'transgression'. This is not as haphazard as it may appear. He has, after all, just given a list of the 'works of the flesh' and now, it seems, he is contemplating the possibility that someone may be found indulging in such a sin. Or had someone already been caught and the facts made known to the apostle? We do not know.

What should the church do in such a circumstance? Paul addresses those 'who are spiritual'. Who are these exactly? There are two possibilities. First, Paul is not above sarcasm in his letters. Possibly he is addressing those who thought themselves very spiritual – a cut above the rest. In effect, he might be saying, 'Those of you who think you are so spiritual, behave with some measure of maturity and understanding.' Perhaps they were ready to condemn and no more? That would be an attitude unbecoming of the Holy Spirit and therefore *unspiritual*. Second, and more likely, Paul may be referring to those Christians who were displaying the fruits of the Spirit mentioned at the close of the last chapter. These were not walking after the flesh but in step with the Spirit. They have a responsibility towards a brother who has fallen.

In a few words, Paul mentions the aim, and the manner, of what needs to be done for their erring brother. The aim is *restoration*. Paul uses the common word for fixing something that is broken (it is used for mending fishing nets in Mark 1:19). The sin of one brother has fractured the body of Christ. The manner is to be *gentle*. Gentleness, Paul has just reminded them, is a fruit of the Spirit to be displayed by every Christian (5:23). It is also one of the few descriptive attributes that Jesus employed about himself (*Matt.* 11:29). The Galatians are to engage in a ministry that is *Jesus-like*! The spirit (Spirit!) of Jesus is to mark the manner of their ministry in restoring a fallen brother.

But *how* exactly is this restoration to be accomplished? Since Paul does not tell the Galatians what they are to do, they must have already had some rudimentary notion of the procedures to be employed. Paul's instruction given in later correspondence with other churches was unknown to them (for example, 1 Corinthians 5:1–5) unless, perhaps, he had already given them some rudimentary instruction.

Probably the words of Jesus were already circulating by word of mouth among Christian communities (there were no written Gospels yet). Was Paul assuming that they knew the words of Jesus in Matthew 18:15–17 about what to do in the case of a 'brother who sins against you'?

It is instructive that Paul is more concerned about addressing the *manner* and *spirit* of discipline than he is to say anything about the *method*. The reason for this is not difficult to work out. Paul is aware that it is all too easy to engage in the condemnation of others from a hypocritical point of view – to see the speck in another's eye when a log hangs from our own (*Matt.* 7:3; *Luke* 6:41). For this reason, Paul warns the Galatians to keep watch on themselves lest they also be tempted (see also 1 Corinthians 10:12). Several pastoral insights seem to be in view:

• Addressing particular sins in others can awaken something that has lain dormant within us for some time.

• Recognizing that fellow Christians may sin in a particular way can lead us to excuse similar sins in our own lives, perhaps especially if the brother in question is known as a 'mature' and 'godly' Christian. If so-and-so can do this, then so can I!

• The devil will seek to lessen the effectiveness of the restoration by ensuring that those engaging in the process of restoration are themselves guilty of similar transgressions.

• We are at our weakest when addressing the sins of another. Self-righteousness and hypocrisy are close at hand in situations of this kind.

• We find condemnation easier than restoration and forgiveness.

When others sin, we need to watch and pray (*Matt.* 26:41; *Mark* 14:38).

## BURDEN-BEARING

Concern for those who have fallen leads on to a consideration of others who carry burdens (verse 2). Again, Paul does not specify what burdens he has in mind, and this implies that he meant *every burden of whatever kind*. He had mentioned earlier the needs of the poor (2:10) and this may be partly in view here. Later, Paul would himself experience the ministry of such burden-bearing. He writes with evident gratitude from his prison in Rome of the way in which the brethren at Philippi had yoked themselves with him and were prepared to experience financial deprivation themselves in order to ease his own burdens (*Phil.* 4:14–15). But no doubt the apostle has in view a greater horizon: there are the ministries of prayer, friendship, and love, to mention just a few. The Christian life is not meant to be lived in isolation. We are intimately joined to one another just as we are intimately joined to Jesus Christ. There is only 'one body' (*Eph.* 4:4).

Bear one another's burdens, the apostle urged, and in this way you will *fulfil the law of Christ*. In a letter in which Paul has had many things to say about the relationship that Christians have to the law, particularly the Old Testament ceremonial law as it relates to circumcision and the food regulations, two questions need addressing: What does Paul mean by 'the law of Christ'? And, more importantly, What does it mean (and why is it necessary) to 'fulfil' the law by engaging in this ministry of burden-bearing?

1. Paul does not use the expression 'the law of Christ' anywhere else. Are we to draw a sharp distinction between the law of Christ and the law of Moses? Is Paul saying that the Christian's rule of life and behaviour is based on the teaching of Christ and has nothing to do with anything that Moses said?

Those drawing sharp distinctions between life in the *New* Covenant and life under the *Old* Covenant have insisted that such is indeed what Paul is saying. But this is far too simplistic. While it is true that certain elements of Old Testament law are no longer in force (the ceremonial law; aspects of the law relating to the civil code of Israel), Paul has nowhere suggested that *all* aspects of the law of Moses – the moral law, or its summary in the Ten Commandments – are nullified by the dawning of the last days in the coming of Jesus Christ. What does Paul mean, then, by the expression *the law of Christ*? Probably no more than the idea that in bearing the burdens of other Christians God's people are actually following a pattern, or principle, embodied by Jesus himself. After all, he bore the burden of our sins (3:13–14). The pattern of life in step with the Spirit is one in which Christ 'lives in me' (2:20).

2. Paul has been concerned to criticize those in Galatia who were insisting upon keeping certain aspects of the ceremonial law. How can he now be keen to speak of the need to *fulfil* the law of Christ (especially since he uses a word to which is added a prefix that suggests *completely* fulfilling the law)? While the apostle is categorically insisting that there is no place for law-keeping as far as justification is concerned, the matter is altogether the opposite whenever sanctification is in view (as here in Galatians 6).

We can *do* nothing in order to be justified. We are not reckoned Christians on the basis of our obedience. Justification is by faith *alone* in Jesus Christ *alone*. But having been brought into a living relationship with Jesus Christ, we are now called upon to live *in step with the Spirit*. This, too, is of the Spirit's doing, but not in such a way that we have no responsibility whatsoever. We are to obey even though our obedience is only effectual because of the help of the Spirit. In the working out of our holiness there is no such thing as being over-scrupulous, although it *is* possible to be scrupulous in an unbiblical way. Fulfilling the law is what it is all about. And for Paul, the summary of that law's demands can be seen in the words and example of Jesus. There is no conflict between Moses and Jesus when it comes to the moral demands of the law. Nor are the demands lessened by the advent of Christ. Indeed, Jesus said, 'unless your righteousness exceeds that of the scribes and Pharisees, you will never enter the kingdom of heaven' (*Matt.* 5:20), adding on another occasion, 'If you love me, you will keep my commandments' (*John* 14:15; 15:10).

## THINKING TOO HIGHLY OF ONESELF

Having warned the Galatians in the opening verse of this chapter of the danger of hypocrisy while ministering to others, Paul now expands on this theme, as if sensing that the Galatians needed more detailed instruction on the danger of a spirit of arrogance and one-upmanship. He speaks of those who thought they were something when in fact they were nothing (verse 3). He warns of the danger of self-deception. When Augustine was asked to summarize what we might call 'the law of Christ', he replied, 'First, humility; second, humility; third humility.' The church is in no way immune to self-promotion and advancement at the expense of others. It is all too easy to make ourselves appear better than we are in the context of the downfall of another. Self-congratulation can easily be the prelude to boasting and pride. And it is in no way clear which is worse in Paul's mind – the original offence of the fallen brother or the conceit of another who seeks to profit from it.

Having just warned the Galatians not to engage in self-congratulation at the expense of another's demise and urging self-examination, Paul now speaks about *boasting* (verses 4–5)!

It could be that Paul has in mind the spirit of self-congratulation that can arise by comparing oneself with a fallen brother, but that would be difficult to reconcile with Paul's urging to boast in 'himself alone and not in his neighbour'. Rather he is saying something different. Here, in verse 4, Paul is thinking of the temptation to take credit for another's holiness! Either way, self-congratulation is the issue, and Paul urges his brothers of the danger of both possibilities.

But Paul elsewhere states that, before God's throne, there is no room for boasting (*Rom.* 3:19, 27). How can he now urge his brothers to boast? How can these things be reconciled? The answer lies further on in the chapter. In verse 14, Paul makes it his aim to boast in nothing except the cross. He therefore cannot possibly be contradicting himself, here in verse 4, just a few verses earlier! Ultimately what Christians boast in is that which the Spirit has brought about in their lives through their union and communion with the Saviour. Live this way, Paul urges: by taking note of what the Holy Spirit has accomplished in you and see it as the fruit of the cross of Christ.

## CARRY YOUR OWN BURDENS!

There is yet another apparent contradiction. In verse 2 he told the Galatians to bear the burdens of others. Now in verse 5 he tells them that they should bear their own burdens!

In fact Paul uses two different words, translated as 'burdens' in verse 2, and 'load' in verse 5. The idea of the first word is of a load too great for one man to carry alone. In verse 5 Paul is thinking of something different. He uses a word that we might render 'backpack'. Paul has in mind that not only *can* it be carried alone, but that it *must* be! Just as it is wrong to ignore the needs of others who are struggling and cannot make it on their own, so it is equally wrong to impose oneself on the kindness of others when the load is relatively light and is our responsibility to carry. Freeloaders (to use the common euphemism) are just as offensive to the apostle as hypocrites!

There may be a connection with what follows in verse 6 where Paul raises the issue of those who 'live off the gospel' – full-time workers who are paid by the church. At first glance, the verse appears totally unconnected with what is said before or after it. At this early stage of the church's existence, a fully-supported ministry was probably relatively rare. Paul himself took no stipend from those to whom he ministered but worked with leather in 'tent-making' to provide income for himself and his needs. The Philippian church was the only one, as far as we know, that sent him financial aid (*Phil.* 4:14-20), even though Jesus had taught that a labourer is worthy of his hire (*Matt.*10:10). And, while it is true that circumstances still exist where it is better to engage in a 'tent-making' ministry, living independently rather than upon the support of others, these are not 'normal' circumstances. The norm, as Paul will increasingly make clear, is that full-time workers in the church should receive their support from their brethren (*catechumens* is the word Paul uses – those who are taught). See 1 Corinthians 9:13–14; 2 Corinthians 11:7-11.

We can only guess why Paul needed to urge such support. Perhaps, if this is indeed the first of his letters to them, he felt the need to begin this instruction to the church from the very outset. Perhaps, also, the Galatian elders whom he had appointed were being criticized by those troublemakers who had necessitated this letter in the first place. Such criticism would lead some to withdraw their support. Having warned in verse 5 that it is all too possible to abuse the generosity and sensitivity of other Christians, demanding more than is due (to such Paul had urged that they carry their own load), it is also necessary to underline the responsibility that the church has to support those who have been set apart for full time ministry in its midst.

# 23

# *Weary in Well-Doing*

*Do not be deceived: God is not mocked, for whatever one sows,
that will he also reap. $^8$ For the one who sows to his own flesh
will from the flesh reap corruption, but the one who sows to the
Spirit will from the Spirit reap eternal life. $^9$ And let us not grow
weary of doing good, for in due season we will reap, if we do not
give up. $^{10}$ So then, as we have opportunity, let us do good to
everyone, and especially to those who are of the household of faith*
(Gal. 6:7–10).

'Do-gooders' has become in our time a euphemism for
hypocrites and meddlesome busybodies. But, in this closing
section of Paul's letter, 'doing good' represents the fruit of the Spirit's
activity in the life of a believer. In fact, without it, there is no evidence
of a transformed heart. Before he elaborates on what this might
mean, Paul engages in a series of motivational statements.

The New Testament provides us with more than one motivation
for doing good. Sometimes the love of God is our motivation, as in
2 Corinthians 5:14, 'For the love of Christ controls us', or, as in the
case of the preaching of some in Philippi, which Paul describes as
having been done 'out of love' (*Phil.* 1:17). Many have argued that
love ought to be the only motivational basis for ethical conduct; that
to do something out of, say, the fear of punishment, is a *less than
Christian* way to live. Some have simplistically represented this as
the difference between life under the Old Covenant (motivated by
fear) and life under the New Covenant (motivated by love). To this
has been added a further observation: that motivation by the fear of

punishment is essentially a return to a 'salvation by works' mentality and a denial of the *grace* of the gospel.

On the face of it, Paul seems to address this very issue when he says: *Do not be deceived; God is not mocked; you reap what you sow.*

The possibility of *deception* is a real one. These Galatian Christians had been duped already by teachers who had questioned the gospel of the apostle Paul, especially his formulation of justification by faith alone. Their arguments over the place of circumcision had sounded especially convincing. Christians can all too easily be 'taken in' by persuasive arguments and charismatic personalities.

Of what were they in danger of being deceived? Two things: one with respect to God and another with respect to themselves.

1. '*God is not mocked.*' Paul uses a very strong word that means 'to turn up the nose in contempt'! Ezekiel describes how in his day some were literally doing that to God (*Ezek.* 8:17). The point is that nothing that we do will go unnoticed by God. He sees everything we do. The motivation here is that the eye of God is upon us at all times, and he sees the moments of hypocrisy, the times of flagrant disregard. The point of saying this is to underline that God is a judge of our actions. It is of the same order of thought as Paul's words to the Corinthians: 'We make it our aim to please him. For we must all appear before the judgement-seat of Christ, so that each one may receive what is due for what he has done in the body, whether good or evil' (*2 Cor.* 5:9-10). The motivation is the judgement of God.

2. '*We reap what we sow.*' The point of this principle is to underline our responsibility for cultivating habits of good behaviour – fruits of the Spirit's activity within our lives. Such fruit will demand resolute activity on our part.

It is a principle, however, that needs to be handled with care! Eliphaz, one of Job's so-called friends, had used this very argument in his opening speech (*Job* 4:8). His point had been to suggest that Job's trials were the result of his own sinful actions; that he only had himself to blame for his current predicament. The whole point of the book of Job is to argue that Eliphaz was utterly wrong! Not that the maxim, 'you reap what you sow' is wrong in itself, but that its application in Job's case was wrong. Job was not suffering because of something he had done. Principles must not be applied unthinkingly. To say, for example, to someone who is suffering, 'Well, you have got what you deserve', may be true. But equally, it may not be. The answer Jesus gave to the disciples' question as to the cause of a man's blindness should be a warning to us: it was not the result of either the man's sin or that of his parents (*John* 9:1–3).

## SOWING AND REAPING

The passage is not as disconnected as it might appear. Having used the metaphor of sowing and reaping, Paul now applies it to the contrast established in chapter 5 between the flesh and the Spirit. If we sow to the flesh we will reap fleshly things. If we sow to the Spirit, we will reap spiritual (Spiritual!) things. One way leads to the bad fruit mentioned earlier, such things as 'sexual immorality, impurity, sensuality, idolatry, sorcery, enmity, strife, jealousy, fits of anger, rivalries, dissensions, divisions, envy, drunkenness, orgies, and things like these' (5:19–21). Those who habitually practise such things 'will not inherit the kingdom of God' (5:21). Or, as Paul now puts it, they 'will reap corruption' (verse 8). Those who, on the other hand, sow to the Spirit, yielding such things as 'love, joy, peace, patience, kindness, goodness, faithfulness, gentleness, self-control' (5:22–23), will reap 'eternal life'.

The contrast could not be starker. No longer is it merely the temporal consequences of what may occur in this life that are in view; these life-styles yield eternal consequences. One path leads to destruction, and another leads to eternal life. As Paul put it in another letter: 'If you live according to the flesh you will die, but if by the Spirit you put to death the deeds of the body, you will live' (*Rom.* 8:13). Even though Paul uses a word, 'destruction,' that conveys the idea of a rotting corpse, he does not intend to suggest that such will in the end be annihilated. Destruction here has an ongoing aspect to it just as its opposite, 'eternal life' does.

Two questions now arise:

1. What are we to make of a motivation that is governed by the fear of judgement? Is this to be deemed unworthy of a fully-fledged

Christian ethic? In addition, is Paul also suggesting that Christians should be motivated by the prospect of reward (eternal life)?

2. Paul has been making a contrast between our *working* and salvation by grace through faith in Jesus Christ. We are not justified by works but by grace. Is he contradicting himself here by saying that, after all, there is something that we *must do* in order to inherit eternal life?

These are important questions – and they are also related to each other. They touch on the relationship of law and grace, God's sovereignty and our responsibility, and justification and sanctification.

In answer to the first set of questions, the motivation of fear needs to be carefully formulated. The judgement of God is meant to make us focus on issues that are outside of this world. It provides our obedience with three qualities: a sense of *perspective* (that all our works are to done, as our forefathers would have said, *sub specie aeternitatis*, in the light of eternity – note the words in verse 9, 'we will reap a harvest'); a sense of *direction* (ultimately it is God we serve, and not each other; still less is it ourselves); a sense of *honesty* (it must pass the scrutiny of God's eye and not just our own).

As for the need to produce works (fruitful lives), Paul is not thinking here of any 'good work' that will in any way merit salvation, but of how we respond to the salvation that is already ours in Christ. We are not to work for our salvation, but having received it as a gift we are *working out our salvation* (*Phil.* 2:12–13). The free gift of salvation is to result in a life that is more and more conformed to the image and likeness of the Saviour (*Rom.* 8:29). The salvation which is given to us works itself out in the totality of our existence: our thinking, willing, feeling, and doing. As someone has put it, 'The entrance fee is nothing at all, but the annual fee is everything we've got!'

## DON'T STOP!

Having spoken of the need to produce the Spirit's fruit, Paul now addresses the issue of *perseverance*: 'Let us not grow weary of doing good' (verse 9). The best intentions fail for lack of resolve and commitment.

There are pertinent reasons why Paul might have thought the Galatians were particularly prone to giving up. Division and dissension can make us give up on people who are seen to be ungrateful and difficult. The coldness of others can often be infectious. Cynicism is a deadly disease of the heart that often arises in the wake of strife. Paul had already hinted earlier, and in another context, how easily professing Christians can change course – having begun one way, they end in another (see also 3:3). There is a need for us to *continue* as we have begun (*Col.* 1:23; *1 Tim.* 2:15).

Similar expressions are found elsewhere in the New Testament: our final *preservation* in the faith (our assurance of eternal life) is dependent upon our ongoing *perseverance* in the faith. We will reap '*if* we do not give up'. Paul writes to the Colossians of God's intention to 'present you holy and blameless and above reproach before him, *if indeed you continue in the faith*' (*Col.* 1:22–23). To Timothy he says, '*if we endure*, we will also reign with him' (*2 Tim.* 2:12). And to the Hebrews he writes, 'we share in Christ, *if* indeed we hold our original confidence firm to the end' (*Heb.* 3:14).

Does the conditionality of these statements imply that a Christian can *fall from grace*? Is Paul undermining the truth of his words in other passages to the effect that having begun in the Christian way, God will ensure its completion (see Philippians 1:6)? Or is he contradicting his emphasis that *nothing* can separate believers from the love of God in Jesus Christ – that an unbreakable link exists between justification and glorification (*Rom.* 8:30)?

Paul recounts cases of apostasy, Christians who began the race but did not finish, and of whose salvation he has no assurance, for example, Hymenaeus and Philetus (*2 Tim.* 2:17); and Demas (*2 Tim.* 4:10). What must be borne in mind at this point is that the New Testament speaks (*can only speak*) of Christians according to their profession of faith.

It does say that a true child of God can never fall away; a true child of God will persevere, shunning sin, killing sinful habits and displaying the fruits of the Spirit. Failure here will lead to certain destruction – *no matter what profession has been made or the degree to which that profession has been credible to others.*

# THE HOUSEHOLD OF FAITH

Having examined the intricacies of some of Paul's pronouncements, we now notice that the section ends with a general exhortation to do good to all, especially those who are 'of the household of faith' (verse 10). The ultimate consideration of our responsibility to other Christians is that we are one family – we live in the same house! We are brothers and sisters. We are obligated to each other because we share a common family identity.

It would be a healthy exercise to ask ourselves a series of questions at this point.

*Question 1*: Am I approaching each new day eager to discover the opportunities in which I may express 'good' as the indicator of the Spirit's presence within my heart? Am I merely content with past attainments?

*Question 2*: Do I confine my attention simply to those who are in the church of Jesus Christ? Am I known among those who are unbelievers as one who 'does good'? Do I have 'a reputation for good works' (*1 Tim.* 5:10)?

*Question 3* : Am I concerned about the material welfare of others, sharing with those who are dependent for their livelihood upon the generosity of their Christian brothers and sisters (see 6:6)? Can I truly say of my 'good' in this area, that it is 'from the heart' (*Eph.* 6:6), and cheerful (*2 Cor.* 9:7)?

The reality – or otherwise – of our communion in the body of Christ will be revealed by our answers.

# 24

## *Only a New Creation Counts*

*See with what large letters I am writing to you with my own hand. [12] It is those who want to make a good showing in the flesh who would force you to be circumcised, and only in order that they may not be persecuted for the cross of Christ. [13] For even those who are circumcised do not themselves keep the law, but they desire to have you circumcised that they may boast in your flesh. [14] But far be it from me to boast except in the cross of our Lord Jesus Christ, by which the world has been crucified to me, and I to the world. [15] For neither circumcision counts for anything, nor uncircumcision, but a new creation. [16] And as for all who walk by this rule, peace and mercy be upon them, and upon the Israel of God.*

*[17] From now on let no one cause me trouble, for I bear on my body the marks of Jesus.*

*[18] The grace of our Lord Jesus Christ be with your spirit, brothers. Amen* (Gal. 6:11–18).

As we come to the closing section of this letter we might expect a number of things: a personal greeting from Paul, or from the 'brothers' mentioned in the opening section (1:2); a desire to see the Galatians again soon; an assurance of his prayers on their behalf, or a request for prayer from them. None of these things appears, and instead what we find are several highly personal remarks together with a restatement of the main theme of the letter. Even the greeting (verse 16) is restricted to those 'who walk by this rule' – no 'to all the saints' here! Is this because the relationship between Paul and the Galatians is strained? Perhaps, but he does call them 'brothers' in the final verse.

## CAPITAL LETTERS

We are now to imagine that visually, something unexpected occurs at this point in the letter. The handwriting suddenly becomes much larger and the reason is that though a secretary (*amanuensis*) wrote the letter on Paul's behalf (a customary practice – Paul employed the help of Luke, Timothy, Tertius, Silas and Sosthenes in other letters), at this point Paul takes a pen in hand and begins to write himself (verse 11). Perhaps he had intended initially just to sign his name, 'Paul', and add a benediction (as occurs in verse 18), but he suddenly feels the need to reiterate what he has been saying in the letter. And there is something very strange about Paul's handwriting! He draws attention to the 'large (capital) letters'.

The reason for the large letters has been the source of endless speculation! Earlier we noted the Galatians' willingness to 'gouge out' their eyes and give them to Paul. Was he suffering from some disease of the eye that caused him to have to write in large letters (4:15)? Was this perhaps the thorn in the flesh which he mentions in 2 Corinthians 12:7? It may equally be that the apostle is saying, 'LOOK, I DON'T WANT YOU TO MISUNDERSTAND WHAT IT IS I AM SAYING TO YOU, SO I AM WRITING TO YOU IN CAPITAL LETTERS!'

## WRONG ON ALL COUNTS!

Paul had made it very clear in chapter 5 that Gentiles who became Christians were not under any obligation to be circumcised: 'Look: I, Paul, say to you that if you accept circumcision, Christ will be of no advantage to you' (5:2). This had been his example in the case of Titus (2:3). For Paul, *nothing* is to be added as a requirement for salvation and acceptance within the household of faith other than faith in Jesus Christ. To do so is to destroy the gospel.

What had been the motivation behind the pressure levelled against Gentile converts for them to be circumcised? At this closing point in the letter Paul directs some blistering accusations against the Judaizers in Galatia who had sought the support of some of the brethren in Jerusalem. It was self-promotion of the worst kind! There were those in Jerusalem – 'influential' is the term Paul uses, but undoubtedly with a great deal of sarcasm (2:2, 6) – who would approve of those Galatians who argued as they did. Later, at the Jerusalem Council (as discussed earlier), these folk in Jerusalem would state the matter in its bluntest form, saying, 'Unless you are circumcised according to the custom of Moses, you cannot be saved' (*Acts* 15:1).

The motivation in Galatia was to 'make a good showing' among those in Jerusalem who would congratulate them for upholding and promoting the orthodox way. In addition to the normal practices of proselytism these Judaizers were particularly targeting Gentile converts (Paul's converts!) and drawing them into their Judaizing ways. Indeed, Paul accuses them of using *force* in their attempts to have Gentiles circumcised (verse 12, though he does not mean physical but moral pressure). Such prizes would have received a double honour when reported in Jerusalem. By such actions they showed their Jewish credentials.

But the motivation is of another sort, too. By such actions they would also avoid being 'persecuted for the cross of Christ' – something Paul himself had not avoided (5:11). In addition, as Paul had suggested earlier, these agitators were insisting upon law-keeping as a requirement to salvation, but this implies an obligation to keep 'the whole law' (5:3), *and this is impossible!* They insist on law-keeping when they 'do not themselves keep the law' (verse 13).

The charge Paul is making is thus fourfold: they were *bullies, sycophants, hypocrites* and *cowards* to boot! Can you feel the tension this must have created when it was read out loud in Galatia?

## BOASTING IN THE CROSS

Paul has raised the issue of boasting – how the Judaizers in Galatia were boasting of their Gentile 'trophies' succumbing to the pressure to be circumcised. Christians, and especially ministers, can do this, too, claiming a true convert as one of their own! Such boasting is ruled out – 'Far be it from me to boast' (verse 14). This is the expression rendered, 'God forbid', in the King James Version (see also 2:17, where it is rendered, in our translation, 'Certainly not!'). Having expanded on the righteousness that comes from obedience to the law in Romans 3, Paul asks, 'What becomes of our boasting?' His answer? 'It is excluded' (*Rom.* 3:27).

Having ruled out any form of self-confident boasting in our own obedience to the law (*Phil.* 3:3–4), Paul now opens the door to the only legitimate boasting a Christian can do: *boasting in the cross of Jesus Christ!*

We might expect Paul to say that he boasts in Jesus Christ, or in the love of God. That would make more sense than to boast of a method of corporal and capital punishment! It is as though he were saying, 'I boast in the gas-chamber', or, 'I boast in the electric chair'! How can anyone *boast* in an instrument of torture and death? How easily we sentimentalize the cross and forget how brutal a form of death it was.

Left uninterpreted the cross of Jesus Christ makes no sense at all – still less would there be any sense in anyone boasting in it. To many in Paul's day (and in our own) the cross signalled the defeat of Jesus Christ. It demonstrated failure! Some have even suggested that the story of the resurrection was 'invented' to provide some sort of gloss on an otherwise depressing story of failure and rejection. How, then, can Paul boast in the cross?

The answer lies in what the cross *means*. And this the New Testament explains in a way that calls forth praise and worship from every Christian. In Galatians 3:13, Paul explained its significance by saying, 'Christ redeemed us from the curse of the law by becoming a curse for us.' On the cross, Christ was *redeeming* us – *paying the ransom price to set us free*. The cross is *propitiatory* – Christ underwent the curse of the broken covenant *in our place* in order to *satisfy* divine justice (see Romans 3:25). Words like *redemption, propitiation, substitution, satisfaction* and *reconciliation* provide the cross with an explanation that makes Paul's boasting of it not only understandable but compulsory. The cross signals the greatness of God's love for us in his determination to save us when the cost was the death of his only Son. 'See what kind of love the Father has given to us . . . (*1 John* 3:1).

## CRUCIFIED

Two consequences emerge as Paul boasts in the cross of Jesus Christ. The first is that 'the world has been crucified to me' (verse 14). What Paul means is that the world (that is the world as a way of life apart from Jesus Christ) has nothing to offer him now that he has Jesus Christ. He found no lasting satisfaction in anything the world had to offer. If we possess the world but do not have Christ, we have nothing. If we have Christ and nothing else, we have everything. Indeed, Paul had come to see the world quite differently. He now understood it as a place under the curse of God and destined for destruction.

Paul adds something else: 'I am crucified to the world.' This is often interpreted as a statement of consecration (in much the same way as the previous statement). It is best, however, to understand him as saying something else here. Paul is not thinking now of how he regarded the world but how the world regarded him. And the world thought of him as a fool – in much the same way as they had regarded Jesus Christ. As far as the world was concerned, Paul was a dead man! He was nothing. A non-entity! His words meant nothing! It was the measure of his identification with the cross of Jesus that the world treated him in the same way as it had dealt with Jesus Christ.

Thoughts of this world produce in the apostle's mind an idea that is only expressed in embryo. He does not develop it. If this world has nothing to offer him and treats him with contempt, what does it matter? God is preparing him (and every Christian) for a new world! In the end, circumcision, to which these trouble-makers in Galatia and Jerusalem had attached such importance, was of no value. What is really important is the new creation that God is going to bring about (verse 15). This new creation has, in effect, already begun in the life of a Christian (see 2 Corinthians 5:17). Something of the end-time reality has broken through into our own existence – a kind of foretaste of the fullness which is to come.

## YOURS SINCERELY, PAUL

As we have already noted, Paul only greets those who 'walk by this rule' and not everyone who professed the faith in Galatia. The issue over circumcision has been an important one, so much so that Paul is excluding those who have insisted upon it from his farewell greeting. But Paul adds, 'and to the Israel of God' – a phrase which has been the cause of much speculation.

Some students of Scripture argue forcefully that Paul is here referring to Jews. Having indicated that unless they believe in Jesus Christ alone they are not saved, he still longs that they would be. As he would later confess: 'For I could wish that I myself were accursed and cut off from Christ for the sake of my brothers, my kinsmen according to the flesh' (*Rom.* 9:3).

Others have believed that what Paul is doing is expanding on what he has said earlier in the sentence. In which case 'Israel of God' and 'those who walk by this rule' are parallel phrases, and both identify the true church of Jesus Christ – made up of converted Jews and Gentiles. In this case, Paul has performed a major shift in his thinking from that which had governed him as a Jew: he sees the New Testament church as a continuation of Old Testament Israel. The church is 'the commonwealth of Israel' (*Eph.* 2:12). For Paul, there is only one plan of salvation and one people of God. Though he has argued for discontinuity as far as the ceremonial aspects of the law of the Old Testament are concerned, other aspects of the law (*and the promises*) remain.

## A MARKED MAN

Why should the Galatians listen to Paul? What evidence is there that anything he says can be trusted? Was he, as so many others had proved to be, a mere charlatan – another preacher eager to extract a living from the gullible and desperate? It is just here that Paul writes something deeply personal. His love for the cross of Jesus Christ had literally marked him out. He bore on his back the 'marks (*stigmata*) of Jesus' (verse 17). Any time the apostle took off his shirt, the cost of discipleship would be visible to all around him. Some of them had perhaps witnessed firsthand the occasion of Paul's beating at Lystra when he had been left at the side of the road as dead (*Acts* 14:19–20). Paul's testimony is that those who would follow Jesus will have a cross at the centre of their lives! Nor is he ashamed of it! He counts it a privilege to suffer for Jesus and would later write, 'Now I rejoice in my sufferings for your sake, and in my flesh I am filling up what is lacking in Christ's afflictions for the sake of his body, that is, the church' (*Col.* 1:24).

## THE BENEDICTION

*The grace of our Lord Jesus Christ be with your spirit, brothers,* writes Paul (verse 18), bringing his letter to a close. As elsewhere, Paul combines a plural pronoun (*your,* plural) with a singular noun (*spirit,* singular). After alluding to the strife and tension in Galatia, it may be that he now wants to think of them as a singular entity – the one body of Christ, who walk according to the 'rule' of the gospel. It was undoubtedly what Paul was praying for. The 'Amen' at the end makes it sound as though this was indeed a prayer on their behalf. It is still an appropriate way for us to pray.

# Group Study Guide

**SCHEME FOR GROUP BIBLE STUDY**
(Covering 13 Weeks)

| STUDY PASSAGE | CHAPTERS |
|---|---|
| 1. Galatians 1:1–9 | 1–2 |
| 2. Galatians 1:10–24 | 3–4 |
| 3. Galatians 2:1–5 | 5 |
| 4. Galatians 2:6–14 | 6–7 |
| 5. Galatians 2:15–21 | 8 |
| 6. Galatians 3:1–14 | 9–10 |
| 7. Galatians 3:15–24 | 11–12 |
| 8. Galatians 3:25–4:7 | 13–14 |
| 9. Galatians 4:8–20 | 15–16 |
| 10. Galatians 4:21–5:6 | 17–18 |
| 11. Galatians 5:7–21 | 19–20 |
| 12. Galatians 5:22–6:6 | 21–22 |
| 13. Galatians 6:7–18 | 23–24 |

This Study Guide has been prepared for group Bible study, but it can also be used individually. Those who use it on their own may find it helpful to keep a note of their responses in a notebook.

The way in which group Bible studies are led can greatly enhance their value. A well-conducted study will appear as though it has been easy to lead, but that is usually because the leader has worked hard and planned well. Clear aims are essential.

## AIMS

In all Bible study, individual or corporate, we have several aims:

1. To gain an understanding of the original meaning of the particular passage of Scripture;
2. To apply this to ourselves and our own situation;
3. To develop some specific ways of putting the biblical teaching into practice.

2 Timothy 3:16–17 provides a helpful structure. Paul says that Scripture is useful for:

(i) teaching us;

(ii) rebuking us;

(iii) correcting, or changing us;

(iv) training us in righteousness.

Consequently, in studying any passage of Scripture, we should always have in mind these questions:

What does this passage teach us (about God, ourselves, etc.)?

Does it rebuke us in some way?

How can its teaching transform us?

What equipment does it give us for serving Christ?

In fact, these four questions alone would provide a safe guide in any Bible study.

## PRINCIPLES

In group Bible study we meet in order to learn about God's Word and ways 'with all the saints' (*Eph.* 3:18). But our own experience, as well as Scripture, tells us that the saints are not always what they *are* called to be in every situation – including group Bible study! Leaders ordinarily have to work hard and prepare well if the work of the group is to be spiritually profitable. The following guidelines for leaders may help to make this a reality.

**Preparation:**

1. Study and understand the passage yourself. The better prepared and more sure of the direction of the study you are, the more likely it is that the group will have a beneficial and enjoyable study.
Ask: What are the main things this passage is saying? How can this be made clear? This is not the same question as the more common 'What does this passage "say to you"?', which expects a reaction rather than an exposition of the passage. Be clear about that distinction yourself, and work at making it clear in the group study.

2. On the basis of your own study form a clear idea *before* the group meets of (i) the main theme(s) of the passage which should be opened out for discussion, and (ii) some general conclusions the group ought to reach as a result of the study. Here the questions which arise from 2 Timothy 3:16–17 should act as our guide.

3. The guidelines and questions which follow may help to provide a general framework for each discussion; leaders should use them as starting places which can be further developed. It is usually helpful to have a specific goal or theme in mind for group discussion, and one is suggested for each study. But even more important than tracing a single theme is understanding the teaching and the implications of the passage.

**Leading the Group:**

1. Announce the passage and theme for the study, and begin with prayer. In group studies it may be helpful to invite a different person to lead in prayer each time you meet.

2. Introduce the passage and theme, briefly reminding people of its outline and highlighting the content of each subsidiary section.

3. Lead the group through the discussion questions. Use your own if you are comfortable in doing so; those provided may be used, developing them with your own points. As discussion proceeds, continue to encourage the group first of all to discuss the significance of the passage (teaching) and only then its application (meaning for us). It may be helpful to write important points and applications on a board by way of summary as well as visual aid.

4. At the end of each meeting, remind members of the group of their assignments for the next meeting, and encourage them to come prepared. Be sufficiently prepared as the leader to give specific assignments to individuals, or even couples or groups, to come with specific contributions.

5. Remember that you are the leader of the group! Encourage clear contributions, and do not be embarrassed to ask someone to explain what they have said more fully or to help them to do so ('Do you mean . . . ?').

Most groups include the 'over-talkative', the 'over-silent' and the 'red-herring raisers'! Leaders must control the first, encourage the second and redirect the third! Each leader will develop his or her own most natural way of doing that; but it will be helpful to think out what that is before the occasion arises! The first two groups can be helped by some judicious direction of questions to specific individuals or even groups (*e.g.* 'Jane, you know something about this from personal experience . . .'); the third by redirecting the discussion to the passage itself ('That is an interesting point, but isn't it true that this passage really concentrates on . . . ?'). It may be helpful to break the group up into smaller groups sometimes, giving each subgroup specific points to discuss and to report back on. A wise arranging of these smaller groups may also help each member to participate.

More important than any techniques we may develop is the help of the Spirit enabling us to understand and to apply the Scriptures. Have and encourage a humble, prayerful spirit.

6. Keep faith with the schedule; it is better that some of the group wished the study could have been longer than that others are inconvenienced by it stretching beyond the time limits set.

7. Close in prayer. As time permits, spend the closing minutes in corporate prayer, encouraging the group to apply what they have learned in praise and thanks, intercession and petition.

NOTE: Though the Study Guide which follows is arranged in thirteen studies, each contains enough material for it to be divided into two studies, making a programme of twenty-six studies in all.

## STUDY 1: Galatians 1:1–9

Read chapters 1 and 2 of this book.

AIM: To cultivate a God-centred way of thinking about the gospel.

1.   Why must Paul defend his credentials in the very opening of his letter to the Galatians? What is significant about Paul being an apostle? How does Paul's position as an apostle bear on the authority of this letter – to the Galatians, and to us today?

2.   Where exactly is Galatia? Why does Paul address the 'churches of Galatia', and how does this reflect the unity of '*the* church of God'?

3.   Paul's greeting is brief and to the point. What can we conclude about the problem Paul will be addressing in the letter from what he does not say in his greeting? What does Paul's description of Christ in verses 3–5 teach us regarding Christ's Person and work? And why would Paul include this in his greeting?

4.   What is Paul's charge against the Galatian church? Why is 'constant vigilance' needed 'in maintaining the truth of the gospel'? How can we today maintain the truth of the gospel?

5.   Take a few moments and write down a definition of sin and of grace. Read Galatians 1:6. What is the gospel about? What is the heart of the problem in Galatia? Do your definitions of sin and grace reflect the way Paul, and therefore the Bible, understands sin and grace? Do you have 'a God-centred way of thinking about man's condition and God's remedy'?

6.   What does Paul mean by a 'different gospel'? What does Galatians 1:6–9 teach about pluralism and relativism? What does Paul mean by 'accursed'? Why can there only be 'one gospel'?

FOR STUDY 2: Read Galatians 1:10–24 and
chapters 3 and 4 of this book.

### STUDY 2: Galatians 1:10–24

AIM: To highlight God's work in conversion.

1. What is the difference between Paul's statements in 1:12 and in 1:1? How are they related?

2. Why was Paul so defensive about his apostolic credentials? What immediate lesson do we learn from Paul's insistence on the gospel? What results from indifference? Do you find yourself ambivalent regarding 'the *essentials*' of the gospel?

3. Compare and contrast the 'what I once was' with the 'what I am now' in the life of Paul? Pause and give praise to God for your conversion (whether you were converted at a young age or as an adult). Pray for the conversion of a friend or family member who does not know Christ as Lord and Saviour.

4. Examine the 'threefold account' of Paul's conversion: predestination, effectual calling, and God's revelation to him of Jesus. Summarize the defence of Paul's preaching. What was Paul doing for the three years after his conversion?

5. Why did Paul travel to Jerusalem? What might have Paul and Peter discussed during Paul's fifteen-day visit?

6. Why was there rejoicing in Judea? What does their response teach us about the way we should respond to the work of the gospel?

FOR STUDY 3: Read Galatians 2:1–5 and
chapter 5 of this book.

## STUDY 3: Galatians 2:1–5

AIM: To focus on the emancipating power of the gospel.

1. 'Why does Paul have to defend himself against the charge that he had learned his message in Jerusalem?' What is at the heart of the issue for Paul in his epistle to the Galatians?

2. When does the author place Paul's second visit to Jerusalem? How is this significant to Paul's dealings regarding circumcision and Jewish ceremonial practices in Galatia?

3. What is the importance of Titus in relation to the controversy in Galatia? How was Titus 'to become the catalyst for doctrinal advance in the fledgling Church's understanding of the gospel and its implications'?

4. What was the importance of circumcision in the Old Testament? Why is circumcision called a 'sign and seal'? What is the relationship between circumcision (and baptism) and one's conversion?

5. Who are 'the interlopers' and why was Paul disturbed by them? What is Paul concerned to protect? What leads the author to write, 'Christian work requires the most intense patience and courage'?

6. Some recent studies have argued for a 'new perspective' on Paul – maintaining that the issue for Paul was not works-righteousness but the identity of the people of God. How is this interpretation a misunderstanding of Paul's use of freedom in this text?

FOR STUDY 4: Read Galatians 2:6–14 and
chapters 6 and 7 of this book.

## STUDY 4: Galatians 2:6–14

AIM: To study how the gospel both unites and divides.

1.  What was the issue over which Paul and the apostles in Jerusalem were 'of one mind'? Were Paul and Peter preaching different gospels? How might God have suited you for specific aspects of ministry in your church?

2.  Why does Paul refer to Peter, James, and John as 'pillars'? What is significant about Paul and Barnabas receiving the 'right hand of fellowship' from the leaders in Jerusalem?

3.  Name some of the effects of materialism upon Christianity? In what way does materialism hinder you from engaging in mercy ministry? What do the apostles teach the Church concerning the priority of serving the poor?

4.  Read the quotation from Martin Luther at the opening of chapter 7. Why does he refer to justification as 'the chief article of Christian doctrine' and how does this relate to the 'face-off' between Paul and Peter?

5.  Discuss the background that ignited the debate on table-fellowship. What is Paul's charge against Peter and Barnabas, and what is the theological principle that concerns him?

6.  How were Peter and Barnabas's actions a denial of the gospel? While you may confess with your mouth the truth of the gospel, are your actions saying otherwise?

FOR STUDY 5: Read Galatians 2:15–21 and
chapter 8 of this book.

## STUDY 5: Galatians 2:15–21

AIM: To understand the difference between justification by faith and justification by faith plus works.

1. In the last study, we noticed that Peter and Barnabas's refusal to engage in table fellowship with Gentiles suggested a 'deep-seated inconsistency' in their understanding of the gospel of grace. Why then does Paul insist on his Jewish credentials in 2:15?

2. Recent studies have introduced a 'new perspective' on Paul and have suggested that we have misunderstood Paul's teaching on justification. Compare and contrast the two interpretations given in this chapter of Paul's use of the phrase 'works of the law'. How has the new interpretation reformulated the way Christians have understood the gospel and atonement?

3. Define 'imputed righteousness.' What is the great exchange? Give biblical support for your answer. How is this important to an understanding of the doctrine of justification by faith alone?

4. Outline and discuss Paul's four statements concerning his relationship to the law. Is Paul speaking of justification or sanctification? What does it mean to be united to Christ? How can Paul say that it is 'Christ who lives in me' and still wrestle with sin? In what way does the Christian live in 'two worlds'?

5. Does our faith call into question God's sovereignty? What is the relationship of union with Christ and justification? What would result if grace could be obtained through law-keeping?

FOR STUDY 6: Read Galatians 3:1–14 and
chapters 9 and 10 of this book.

## STUDY 6: Galatians 3:1–14

AIM: To examine the promise and blessing of Abraham.

1. What are the three vital elements of Paul's preaching? What is the difference between the content of Paul's preaching and the content of the false teaching Paul was confronting?

2. The NT speaks of conversion from two perspectives: the Holy Spirit is received and the Holy Spirit is given. What is the relationship between these two? How is the Holy Spirit received? Does the law have a place in the process of sanctification? What comparison is Paul making between 'flesh' and 'Spirit'?

3. Why does Paul use Abraham as an illustration of justification by faith alone? What is the importance of Genesis 15:6? What does Paul's use of Genesis 15:6 suggest about the doctrine of the inerrancy of Scripture? What two issues are settled by the example of Abraham?

4. Read Deuteronomy 27 and 28. What conclusion does Paul draw about the law? What is the scope of his use of the term 'law'? Is he only referring to the Mosaic Law? Support your answer from Scripture.

5. Discuss the antithesis between law and faith. What dilemma does Leviticus 18:5 produce? What function does 'insistence on obedience to the law' serve? What is the 'curse' that Paul refers to in 3:13? Why is this important for our understanding of our redemption?

6. Define the following terms: redemption, penal substitution, and satisfaction. Discuss how each of these truths are vital for a biblical understanding of the gospel. How is the blessing of Abraham fulfilled?

FOR STUDY 7: Read Galatians 3:15–24 and
chapters 11 and 12 of this book.

## STUDY 7: Galatians 3:15–24

AIM: To become aware of the role and purpose of the law.

1.  In the light of Paul's argument that Jesus was the fulfilment of the promise of Abraham, other questions arise: What about the Mosaic covenant? Is Paul pitting Moses against Christ? Or Moses against Abraham? How does the biblical notion of 'covenant' help to answer these questions?

2.  Define and distinguish between 'promise' and 'promises', and 'seed' and 'seeds'. To whom does the inheritance of the children of Abraham belong?

3.  Why are Paul's comments about the Gentiles shocking? Why are 'many of the statements made by the apostle . . . with respect to the law . . . deeply troubling'? Is Paul an antinomian? Give biblical support for your answer.

4.  What are the negative and positive aspects of the law? What is the relationship of the law to justification? Outline and explain (in writing, or with others in your group) the five aspects of Paul's phrase in this chapter: 'the law was added because of our transgressions'.

5.  What is the pedagogical use of the law? You may want to spend a few moments in your personal devotion writing down specific sins that you need to repent of and seeking God's forgiveness in the Lord Jesus Christ.

6.  What is the importance of Paul's reference to 'angels'? Who is the mediator? How are we to understand the phrase 'when faith came'?

FOR STUDY 8: Read Galatians 3:25–4:7 and
chapters 13 and 14 of this book.

## STUDY 8: Galatians 3:25–4:7

AIM: To develop an understanding of the doctrine of adoption.

1.  Stress has been laid upon the continuity of the Old and New Testaments. 'There is one way of salvation, one faith, operating throughout' both testaments. In what way is there discontinuity or development from the Old Testament to the New?

2.  Theologically, what does baptism represent, especially in reference to Jesus' work on the cross? Define the terms 'sign' and 'seal', and how do these terms relate to water baptism?

3.  What does Paul mean by the phrase 'put on Christ'? Wherein does the assurance of our adoption as sons and daughters of God lie? How can Paul announce that 'there is neither Jew nor Greek', and what implications does this teaching have on the unity of the Church?

4.  What is the fundamental misunderstanding of the law's relationship to justification, which Paul is attacking? Outline the three similes Paul uses to describe the law.

5.  Discuss the three applications the author makes from 4:2. How are we to understand the phrase 'fundamental principles'? What are the benefits of our sonship? Read Romans 8:15–17 and Galatians 4:6. How are we to understand the activity of crying 'Abba! Father!'? Is it an act of the believer or of the Holy Spirit?

6.  What is at the heart of our adopted status? What does 4:4–5 teach about the substitutionary work of Jesus? What two aspects of Christ's relationship to the law are important for a biblical understanding of the phrase 'born under the law'? Spend a few moments to thank God for the substitutionary and satisfactory work of Jesus Christ.

FOR STUDY 9: Read Galatians 4:8–20 and
chapters 15 and 16 of this book.

### STUDY 9: Galatians 4:8–20

AIM: To reject legalism and pursue Christlikeness.

1.  Read Jeremiah 31:31–34. What 'forms the distinguishing feature of the Old and New Covenant administrations'?

2.  What is Paul's concern regarding the danger that these new Christians were facing? What does the phrase 'elementary principles' mean? What are some consequences and dangers of legalism?

3.  Why does Paul change the tone of his letter to the Galatians? What does he mean when he urges the Galatians to be like him? What lessons do we learn from this as to how we should encourage and exhort other Christians towards godliness?

4.  Why had Paul suddenly become an enemy to the Galatians (verse 16)? Outline the various perspectives and interpretations of the phrase 'they want to shut you out' (verse 17). Which interpretation best fits the context of Galatians 4?

5.  What is Paul's pastoral concern for the Galatians? Spend a few moments to pray that God, by the Holy Spirit, would make you more Christlike (cf. Rom. 8:29), and pray for someone you know that Christ might be 'formed' in them.

FOR STUDY 10: Read Galatians 4:21–5:6 and
chapters 17 and 18 of this book.

## STUDY 10: Galatians 4:21–5:6

AIM: To enjoy the freedom that is found in Christ.

1. Why does Paul refer again to Abraham? According to Paul, what is the point of the Hagar/Sarah story? And how does this story illustrate the two views of justification operating in Galatia?

2. Compare and contrast Hagar and Sarah. What two theologies does this 'allegory' illustrate?

3. Compare the actions of those who are 'in Christ' with those who are 'severed from Christ.' How is Jesus 'the great Liberator'? What is the slavery that we are in bondage to?

4. Trace the theme of freedom in the book of Galatians. From what or whom are we freed? How was life under the Old Covenant restrictive in comparison to the New? Is the law completely abolished? How does a relationship based on grace bring about freedom?

5. What is the eschatological aspect of our freedom? Who are the 'we' in verse 5? What is the relationship of the gospel triad of faith, hope, and love? Do you find yourself growing in your love for Christ, for other Christians, and for the lost? Are you eagerly awaiting the return of the Lord Jesus?

FOR STUDY 11: Read Galatians 5:7–21 and
chapters 19 and 20 of this book.

## STUDY 11: Galatians 5:7–21

AIM: To consider hindrances to the Christian life, to aim at putting particular sins to death, and to strive towards personal holiness.

1. Is the Christian life a sprint or a marathon? Why? Where do we find confidence amidst the 'obstacles and hindrances' of life?

2. Who exactly is troubling the Galatians? What is it that lies before the person or persons that hindered the Galatians? What implication can we learn from Paul's warning concerning those who oppose the gospel, and even persecute those who believe the gospel?

3. Read 1 Corinthians 7:17–20. What is Paul's view of circumcision? Why would Paul oppose circumcision in the case of Titus and agree to circumcision in the case of Timothy?

4. Compare and contrast the way of the flesh and the way of the Spirit. How do these 'two spheres' affect the Christian life? What is the relationship between 'definitive' and 'progressive' sanctification? Does Paul equate 'flesh' and 'physical'? Explain. Is everything physical (non-spiritual) to be considered evil?

5. 'What happens when I fail to win the struggle against the flesh? Will that mean my certain condemnation?' In what way does the Holy Spirit lead the Christian?

6. 'Sins have names!' Outline the four categories of sins in verses 19–21. Take a few moments in your personal devotion and list personal sins that you are struggling with, and ask God to help you put those sins to death (cf. Rom. 8:13).

7. How can Paul state that 'disobedience banishes from the kingdom [of God]'? Is Paul teaching works-righteousness? Is Paul referring to justification or sanctification? How does Paul's stress on personal holiness guard against 'easy-believism'?

FOR STUDY 12: Read Galatians 5:22–6:6 and chapters 21 and 22 of this book.

## STUDY 12: Galatians 5:22–6:6

AIM: To reflect on Jesus as the pattern of Christian living.

1. Contrast the 'works of the flesh' and the 'fruit of the Spirit.' What is the chief characteristic of holiness? Does the 'constant effort and diligence' needed to crucify the flesh suggest that sanctification is entirely our work?

2. What does the phrase 'walk by the Spirit' in verse 25 mean? Define the terms 'mortification' and 'vivification.' How do these terms relate to the process of your sanctification?

3. Outline the three categories of the 'fruit of the Spirit'. Why is it significant that the first group begins with 'love'? If Paul's list is a description of Jesus Christ, take a few moments and write down the several ways in which Jesus exemplifies the 'fruit of the Spirit'. Give biblical support for your answers. How do you measure up to this list? In what areas do you need to grow?

4. In the opening of chapter 6, to whom is Paul referring when he addresses 'you who are spiritual'? What is the 'aim, and manner, of what needs to be done for the erring brother' in Galatia? What are some possible personal and corporate benefits of seeking the restoration of an 'erring brother'? What should be our response when we see others sin?

5. What does Paul mean by 'the law of Christ'? What does it mean (and why is it necessary) to 'fulfil' the law by engaging in the ministry of 'burden-bearing'?

6. St Augustine once summarized the Christian life as consisting of: 'First, humility; second, humility; third, humility'. How does this relate to Paul's encouraging of the Galatians to boast? Discuss Paul's use of 'burdens' in verse 2 and 'load' in verse 5.

FOR STUDY 13: Read Galatians 6:7–18 and
chapters 23 and 24 of this book.

## STUDY 13: Galatians 6:7–18

AIM: To boast in nothing except the cross of Jesus Christ.

1.   List some biblical motivations for doing good? Support your answers with Scripture.  In what way are the phrases 'God is not mocked' and 'we reap what we sow' motivational?  Are the motivations of 'fear of judgment' and 'prospect of reward' worthy of a 'fully-fledged Christian ethic'?  Is Paul suggesting that 'there is something that we must do in order to inherit eternal life'?

2.   What is the relationship between our 'final preservation in the faith' and our 'ongoing perseverance in the faith'?  Does a person's profession of faith guarantee perseverance?  Can a genuine Christian lose his or her salvation?

3.   Why are we obligated to serve other Christians?  Answer the serious of questions at the end of chapter 23.

4.   As this epistle comes to an end, 'What was the motivation behind the pressure levelled against Gentile converts for them to be circumcised?'  Compare and contrast the boasting of the Judaizers with the boasting of Paul.  What does it mean to 'boast in the cross'?

5.   What two consequences emerge as Paul boasts in the cross of Jesus Christ?  What is the relationship of the Christian to the world?

6.   What does Paul mean in 6:16 by the phrase 'Israel of God'? Support your answer from the book of Galatians and other Scripture texts.  What does Paul's statement, 'I bear on my body the marks of Jesus', teach us about the Christian life?

7.   As this study of the book of Galatians comes to an end, has your understanding and love for the gospel grown?  Have you found yourself more aware of the dangers of works-righteousness?  Spend a few moments in prayer for the salvation of someone you know who is not a Christian, and ask God to enable you to boast in nothing except the cross of Jesus Christ.

# FOR FURTHER READING

The following books are recommended for the study of Galatians:

MARTIN LUTHER, *Commentary on Galatians* (many translations and editions; an edition in contemporary English was published by Kregel in 1987).

JOHN CALVIN, *Sermons on Galatians*, Edinburgh: Banner of Truth, 1997 (originally published in 1563).

JOHN BROWN, *Galatians* (Geneva Series of Commentaries), Edinburgh: Banner of Truth, 2001 (Originally published 1853).

WILLIAM HENDRIKSEN, *Galatians and Ephesians* (New Testament Commentary), London: Banner of Truth, 1969.

# The **Let's Study** Series

If you have enjoyed *Let's Study Galatians* and found it helpful, you will be interested in other titles from this series of books for personal and group Bible Study from the Banner of Truth Trust.

*Let's Study Matthew* by Mark E. Ross

*Let's Study Mark* by Sinclair B. Ferguson

*Let's Study Luke* by Souglas Milne

*Let's Study John* by Mark G. Johnston

*Let's Sudy Acts* by Dennis Johnson

*Let's Study 1 Corinthians* by David Jackman

*Let's Study 2 Corinthians* by Derek Prime

*Let's Study Ephesians* by Sinclair B. Ferguson

*Let's Study Philippians* by Sinclair B. Ferguson

*Let's Study 1 & 2 Thessalonians* by Andrew W. Young

*Let's Study Hebrews* by Hywel R. Jones

*Let's Study 1 Peter* by William Harrell

*Let's Study 2 Peter and Jude* by Mark G. Johnston

*Let's Study the Letters of John* by Ian Hamilton

*Let's Study Revelation* by Derek Thomas

Series Editor: **Sinclair B. Ferguson**, Redeemer Seminary, Dallas, Texas.

The books in this series are written in a straightforward way to help ordinary Christians understand and apply Scripture. They are ideal for personal use or for families, and feature additional material for Bible study groups.

For more information about our publications, or to order, please visit our website.

## THE BANNER OF TRUTH TRUST

3 Murrayfield Road,       P O Box 621, Carlisle,
Edinburgh EH12 6EL     PA 17013,
UK          USA

www.banneroftruth.co.uk